A COMPACT SURVEY OF
ISLAMIC CIVILIZATION

A COMPACT SURVEY OF
ISLAMIC CIVILIZATION

Dr. Muhammad Hedayetullah

authorHOUSE®

AuthorHouse™
1663 Liberty Drive
Bloomington, IN 47403
www.authorhouse.com
Phone: 1-800-839-8640

Published by AuthorHouse   09/18/2012

ISBN: 978-1-4772-4001-4 (sc)
ISBN: 978-1-4772-4002-1 (e)

Library of Congress Control Number: 2012911956

CONTENTS

Dedicated to my beloved wife

AL–HAJJ FARIDUNNAHAR

ABOUT THE AUTHOR

Dr. Muhammad Hedayetullah has an energetic and dynamic academic life: he started his academic life in Muslim religious education. He first attended the Arabic-Islamic institution, Madrasah-i-'Alia, Dhaka, Bangladesh, whence he obtained his first Masters degree in Islamic Tradition (<u>hadith</u>, M. M.—<u>mawlana</u>). Then switching to the English system of education, he obtained his B. A. (Hon.) and a second Masters degree in Islamic History and Culture from Dhaka University, Bangladesh.

With a Ford Foundation Scholarship, he studied at the Institute of Islamic Studies, McGill University, Montreal, Quebec, Canada, whence he obtained his third Masters degree in Islamic Studies. Then changing the course of his academic line, he moved to Hamilton, Ontario, Canada, where, with a scholarship of the Government of Ontario, he studied at McMaster University and obtained his PhD. degree in Comparative Religion (World Religion).

The author has a teaching career of about 38 years beginning in different colleges in Bangladesh as a lecturer in Islamic History and Culture. Before coming to the McGill University, he was a Research Associate at the Institute of Islamic Research, Karachi, Pakistan. As a teaching Associate, he taught Comparative Religion at McMaster University. He was a Lecturer of Islamic Studies at the Lancaster University, England. Then back in Canada, he joined as a Research Fellow at the Institute of Islamic Studies, McGill University. Finally, he taught for 25 years at Vanier College, Montreal, as a Professor of Comparative Religion and Humanities.

To his credit, there are some books and articles published in scholarly journals. His last book entitled **Unity and Diversity in World's Living Religions: A Compact Survey** was published by Trafford Publishing, United States of America, in 2010.

Dr. Muhammad Hedayetullah may be reached at his e-mail address **hedayet_kutir@yahoo.com** and via telephone/fax at **1-514-747-6695**. You can also visit his Facebook page at

ACKNOWLEDGEMENTS

For writing this book arose inspiration both from within myself and from my wife, Al-Hajj Faridunnahar, and my son, Fuad Ikram, who helped me for all technical matters without which I could not have completed this book, especially with my present knee problem. As for my wife's contributions in writing this book, I must express my gratitude to her for taking care of the whole family affairs, in and out of the home, plus taking care of me, in particular, because of my knee condition which has been going on for more than a year now. She could not go to Bangladesh because of my knee problem even after my mother-in-law's death. May Almighty grant her a long and healthy life.

The next persons whose well-wishes also inspired me to write this book are my affectionate daughter Nishat Sultana and her husband Dr. Navid Zargari, academically a brilliant student and as a person a gentleman of uncommon level; and my two lovely grand daughters Safa and Shadi Zargari. I wish for their best future. Apart from the members of my family, the persons who helped me to complete this book are my brother-like Mohammad Ibrahim for technical help and Dr. Angelika Maeser Lemieux, who has spent her valuable time in reviewing and suggesting some changes to make a better sense.

I thank all of them from the core of my heart. May Almighty grant them all good health and long life.

FOREWORD

In **<u>A Compact Survey of Islamic Civilization</u>**, Dr Muhammad Hedayetullah has once again shown himself to be capable of condensing a great deal of information and scholarship into an accessible and interesting format for the general reader as well as the person with a background in Islam. Both the novice and the adept will benefit from his erudition and ability to explain complex topics in a straightforward and engaging manner. The reader will not come away without having a deeper and clearer understanding of the elements that have gone into creating Islamic Civilization.

In six chapters Dr. Hedayetullah skillfully surveys the wide-ranging geographic presence of Muslims and their formidable population growth, the spread of the Islamic religion, the influence of the pre-Islamic beliefs and values of the Bedouins, the Hebrews, and early Christian sects, the life of the Prophet Muhammad, the fundamental principles of Islam, the <u>Shari'a,</u> Muslim family and social life, and the mystical Sufi sects.

Professor Hedayetullah presents the main events of the Prophet Muhammad's life, such as his youth, his family life, his mystical experiences, the revelation of the Qur'an in stages, his followers, important battles led and fought by him, the growth of the Community, and the spread of the faith beyond Arabia, and its relationship to other belief systems. The spiritual values of Islam are shown to be the dynamic force that enabled it to spread the Divine Message of Unity. Dr. Hedayetullah sees in this a liberalizing influence, a call to unity and peace among all peoples. Unfortunately, dissensions within the Community did break out at times and led to different emphases among various groups, which are explained by the author.

Nowadays when the public perception of Islamic Civilization is often distorted and inaccurate due to the War on Terror since 9/11 and Western fears of Muslims, it is most important for the authentic principles of the faith to be understood. People need to know what the Prophet stood for, what his legacy was, and what Islamic institutions such as the law and the family entail. Dr. Hedayetullah's elaboration of the Five Pillars or fundamental principles and their application to daily life, and the Shari'ah and its application to conduct, will help to promote a clearer and sympathetic understanding for readers. The influence of these fundamentals and laws on the family and social life of Muslims in different times and places is interestingly investigated. For Islam, as well as other faiths, modernization and tradition in the contemporary world bring challenges to individuals and communities.

Moreover, the contribution of the mystical wing of Islam, Sufism, deserves wider dissemination since mysticism is generally viewed as a very esoteric study that removes men from the mundane life. However, this is not the case, as Dr. Hedayetullah shows. Ability to get along with, to dialogue with, and to respect other faith traditions, has been a hallmark of the mystics and their followers; they are perhaps the best ambassadors of Comparative Religion and pointers to the future when—we hope—religious strife, narrow dogmatism, and sectarianism will have declined and ceased to contribute to wars. Despite their emphasis upon love, the Sufis nevertheless often elicited hostile reactions from more dogmatic and strict interpreters of faith, and the author exposes some of these conflicts. Dr. Hedayetullah further explores the manner in which Islam was spread by both sword and by love, the warriors and the mystics. The latter's ability to win the hearts of the peoples among whom the Muslim armies moved had a civilizing effect and built bridges between different religions.

Finally, I would like to direct readers of this book to Dr. Hedayetullah's previous books (noted elsewhere in this book) so that taken together they may be seen as making his important contribution to an understanding of Islam in all its many fascinating aspects. This, his last volume, will certainly prove to be a fitting contribution to a long labor of love and intellect, his scholarly expertise, and his commitment to disseminating knowledge. I wish to take this opportunity to thank him for his labours and to wish you, the reader, much benefit and pleasure in reading it.

Dr. Angelika Maeser Lemieux
St. Laurent, Quebec
June 4th, 2012

PREFACE

Islam is one of the Semitic Religions thus one of the greatest religions of the world, and it is not easy to present a complete description of this religion in a Compact Survey, as this book is. It is also not easy to understand the practical life of the Muslims without some knowledge of their religious-social life. For that, one needs to have a complete understanding of the principal institution of Islam. A compact exposition of Muslim institutions covers at least important aspects of Arab-Muslim life. Keeping in mind these facts, I have tried to deal with the origin, background, and the rise of Islam; the dogmas and the superstitions of the faith; the sources and practice of Muslim law, the family life; and Sufism. It packs an immense amount of information even though there are still other aspect to be dealt with.

Concerning the life of the Prophet, it is well-known that Muhammad b. ʿAbdullah was born about 570 C.E. in Mecca (*al-Makkah*), the son of a Korashite family. Orphaned early, he grew up under the care of his nearest relatives. His father had already died so he was brought up by his nearest relatives—his grandfather and his uncle. He was a shepherd during his boyhood age. It is also reported that unlike other boys, Muhammad was thoughtful, rather than playful. At the age of about twenty-five, he became the business adviser of a famed widow named Khadija, who was fifteen years his senior. Eventually he became her third husband. We do not know much about his early religious life. He seems, however, to have begun early to meditate on the values of life, and to have had an unusually nervous, "high-strung constitution."

At the age of forty, he started receiving the divine messages

For publication, please contact the author:
Dr. Muhammad Hedayetullah
359 Gratton Street
Ville Saint-Laurent
Quebec, Canada
H4M-2C8
Telephone: 514-747-6695
Email: hedayet_kutir@yahoo.com
Facebook:

CHAPTER 1

INTRODUCTION

THE BACKGROUND (Semitic Origin)

The word Islam is a derivation of three letters, I. S. L., which mean "peace". Further, the word Islam, as a technical term to denote or stand for the system of religion or belief and rituals based on the Qur'an, is derived from the repeated use of the verb <u>aslama</u> ("submit" oneself) "in the Kuran to denote the characteristic attitude of the true believer in relation to God."(1) In <u>Sura</u> 3.19 it is strongly stated: "The [true] religion with Allah is al-Islam"; further, in <u>Sura</u> 5. 3: it is finally stated on the day of the Farewell Pilgrimage (<u>hajjatul wida'</u>): "This day have I perfected your religion for you and completed My favour unto you, and have chosen for you as religion AL-ISLAM"

Combining the two above-mentioned words "peace" and "submission", one obtains the following definition: a Muslim is one who is peaceful and submissive to the Will of Almighty Allah. In other words, a Muslim who has submitted to Allah must be a peaceful person. In this sense, Islamic principles in human relations are Universal precepts for peace and happiness.

(1) <u>Speak to the people</u>. There is nothing so nice as a cheerful word of greeting.

(2) <u>Smile at people</u>. It takes 72 muscles to frown, and only 14 to smile.

(3) <u>Call people by name</u>. The sweetest music to anyone's ears is the sound of his own name.

(4) <u>Be friendly and helpful</u>. If you want friends, you must be one.

(5) <u>Be cordial</u>. Speak and act as if everything you do is a joy to you.

(6) <u>Be genuinely interested in people</u>. You can like almost every body if you try.

(7) <u>Be generous with praise</u> and cautious with criticism.

(8) <u>Be considerate</u> with the feelings of others. There are usually three sides to a controversy:

Yours, the other fellows', and the right side.

(9) <u>Be eager</u> to lend a helping hand. Often it is appreciated more than you know.

(10) <u>Add to this</u> a good sense of humour, a huge dose of patience and a dash of humility. This combination will open many doors and the rewards will be enormous.

It may be mentioned here that "The infinitive Islam occurs in eight passages, in some of which it may already be emphasised in this technical sense, e. g. <u>Sura</u> 3.19; "The [true] religion with God is Islam", and in 5.3, "This day have I perfected your religion for you and completed My favour unto you, and have chosen for you as religion AL-ISLAM.", as mentioned above.

Through a comprehensive analysis of Islam, it becomes clear that it is a system of religion which encompasses religious-social, ethical-moral and political aspects of a Muslim. In other words, a Muslim must be an all-rounded practical person.

Semitic Origins: Islam, like Judaism and Christianity, is of the stock of Semitic tradition beginning from Noah (Ar. Nuh). These people are also descendants of another well-known Semitic prophet, Abraham (ibrahim), from his two sons, Ishmael and Isaac (isma'iland ishaq). In light of the above historical facts, John L. Esposito says, "Islam stands in a long line of Semitic prophetic religious traditions that shares an uncompromising monotheism, and belief in God's revelation, His prophets, ethical responsibility and accountability, and the Day of Judgement. Indeed, Muslims, like the Jews and Christians, are the children of Abraham since they trace their origin back to him. Islam's historic religious and political relationship to other Semitic peoples, mentioned above, has remained strong throughout history."(2) There is another way to know the religion under our study: Semitic religions are also called positive religions, because "they did not grow up like the systems of ancient heathenism, under the action of unconscious forces operating silently from age to age, but trace their origin to the teachings of great religious innovators, who spoke as the organs of a divine revelation, and deliberately departed from the traditions of the past."(3) It is also emphasised by some historians that like Judaism, Islam is also a national religion with universal claims: "Mohammed, the Prophet of Arabia, considered himself to be perfecting the work of Moses and Jesus, and proclaiming the newest Covenant after the Old and New Covenant."(4)

After stating the Semitic background of Islam, let us say a few words on the nature and characters of Islam as a complete system of Muslim life. In this respect it should be stated emphatically that Islam as a way of life is neither a carbon copy of any previous system or civilization nor a complete innovation, but an admixture of both old and new elements. Thus, to make an objective study of Islam in the light of the above-mentioned statement, we would like to consider the dynamic and flexible history of Islam to examine how much it has absorbed in the course of its beginning and development in relation to both Arab or Semitic and non-Semitic cultures. It should be emphasised that original Islam was a compact system of the Muslim Community (ummatulmuslimin), as the Prophet Muhammad got it from God (Allah), based on unity, loving, sharing, and caring, notwithstanding later divisions. Thus, emphasising the value of unity, T. W. Arnold says, "Nevertheless, adherents of the different sects were still regarded as Muslims (a point of practical importance in view of the mutual exclusion of Muslims and unbelievers from inheritance . . .)."(5)

However, followers of different sects or groups were still regarded as Muslims ("a point of practical importance in view of the mutual exclusion of Muslims and unbelievers from inheritance" (Arnold, op. cit.; SEI). In this connection, it should be mentioned that the Shi'a groups gradually divided into as many as twelve groups, like the Christian groups, even though they all live in peace, but the only group which was excluded unanimously was that of the Zindiqs (cf. articles "Shi'a" and "Zindik", SEI).

Foundations of Islam: Islam is based on five fundamental principles (pillars), viz. (1) Faith (iman): There is no god but Allah; (2) Obligatory Prayers (salat) of five times a day (cf. art. "salat", SEI); (3) Poor Tax (zakat), obligatory on rich Muslims only (cf. art. "zakat", SEI); (4) Fasting (sawm) in the lunar month of Ramadan (cf. art. "sawm", SEI); and (5) Pilgrimage ("hajj"), binding on rich Muslims (cf. SEI). In the light of these fundamental principles, obligatory on all Muslims, with some exceptions, as stated above, it is stated emphatically that Islam is a system of religion which consists of both faith and works.

The wider significance given to the word 'Islam' which is in use, as a cultural complex, adopting a specific political system, and legal and social traditions, which in use in modern Muslim practice, may be due partly to the adoption of Western terminology, but also underlies the usual concept of the Dar al-Islam, as opposed to non-Muslim communities.

Expansion of Islam: During the post-prophetic era, when the Muslims were forced into wars, as the Qur'an says (2. 190-94, 216f.), it was bound to enter on a course of expansion, first through conquests within the Arabian Peninsula, then outside of it by the means of both conquests and trader-missionary and sufi preaching. Considering the spread of the Arab-Muslim population, there was an eastward expansion from the central region, across the Indian Ocean, and by the middle of the eighth century Arab traders had gone as far as China and were present in large numbers in Canton. Arab traders' settlements were found scattered throughout the Malaya Archipelago, and at different historical periods small groups had established themselves on the coasts of India, and individual Arabs went to most parts of the Muslim world. It may be stated that in the course of its expansion, Islam dynamically and liberally absorbed many non-Arab foreign elements of all kinds. Thus, commenting on the multi-dimensional nature of Islam, one writer says: "The acceptance of Islam as a religion by men of many different races shows that this vision has a high degree of universality."(6)

There are large Muslim populations in the following countries: To continue the farther expansion of Islam, the Malay Peninsula and Archipelago were conquered by the Muslims in twelfth century of the Christian era and now are populated by an overwhelming Muslim majority. From Arabia through the Central Asian region and the Indian subcontinent of today's Bangladesh, India, and Pakistan, Islam spread along the important trade route to Java and the other islands of the Archipelago. Today, Indonesia is the largest Muslim country of the world with over 280 million people. There is a rapid increase in the process of conversion to Islam from the remaining non-Muslim population that still non-Muslim. There is a large Muslim population in the Philippine Islands.

On the mainland of China, there is a large Muslim population, estimated at 10% of China's total population; Xinjiang province, China's largest and an once-independent country, is a land with a majority Muslim population, with the right to decide its political future; this territory would be an overwhelming Muslim majority country.

In Russia, there is also a considerable number of Muslim population although the exact figure is not available. Russia has also a Muslim majority province, the Caucasus where the people have been fighting for independence for long time. In Tibet, there are believed to be close to more than 100,000 Muslims, most of them are settlers from China and Kashmir. There is a good number of Muslim population in Japan mainland with building mosques; there are also Muslim populations in Formosa, in Manchuria and in Mongolia.

Next to Asia, Africa is the continent where a large number Muslims live in their independent countries, of which Sudan (lately divided between Muslim and Christian territories) was the largest country. Other African Muslim countries are Algeria, Egypt, East Africa, Libya, Nigeria, French Equatorian Africa, Morocco, Tunisia, and there are other West African smaller Muslim countries (colonies). Among the Bantus, Islam has been progressing slowly but surely. In Uganda, Kenya, Tanganyika (including Zanzibar), and Nyasaland. In South Africa, Comores and Madagascar, there are large number of Muslims living in peace and prosperity.

There are Muslims all over the continent of Europe particularly in France and Spain, the latter being an important part of the Muslim Empire until the 16th century A. D. and the former is the home of over 6 million Muslims today. The Muslim population in England has been increasing continuously. There are Muslims in Tataristan, in Bashkiria, in the Crimea and in Ciscaucasia. In Finland, in Lithuania, in Poland there are Muslims. In the former Balkans, the Turkish Muslims returned after 1923 to Asia, leaving a large number of Muslims in Greece, in Bulgaria, in Rumania, in Yugoslavia, and in Albania which has recently become an independent Muslim country. There are also Muslim populations in Belgium and Luxemburg and all over Europe.

On the north and south American continents: U.S.A., Mexico, Brazil, Argentina, Surinam, Trinidad, Jamaica and Canada, there are a considerable number of Muslims—both newcomers and their families with mosques built everywhere, and the Friday congregational prayer is held.

In Oceania: on the continent of Australia, Newzealand and Fiji Island there is a good number of Muslim population.

Muhammad (d. 632 C. E.) ibn 'Abdullah was the Prophet, thus was the recipient of the revelations to him—the Qur'n for the Arab people, to begin with. According to Islamic belief, however, the revelation is not a mystery or secret thing of salvation, but mainly as a set of huqm (instruction) on how to live a life of rahmat (blessedness).

Pre-Islamic Arabs had many tribal cults whence the Prophet took a few elements, for instance, belief in jinn, iblis, spirits and devils arising out of the severe heat of the desert. He also took over some pre-Islamic or ancient Arab cults such as the "fetishistic" or inanimate cult of the Blackstone known as the Ka'ba (cube) in Mecca. The god of the sanctuary was popularly known as the "master of the house"—the "god" of the ka'ba. The place where the ka'ba is located had been inhabited since the time immemorial by the Qurayesh tribe, to which the Prophet Muhammad belonged. Every year it celebrated with pomp and pride the pilgrimage to that Cube, which was also the site of the biggest fair in Central Arabia.

As for the influences which played an important role in the formulation of the life of the Prophet Muhammad, in addition to his native land, the main influences upon Islam were Judaism and Christianity—the other two Semitic religions based primarily on the Unity of God. It is well-known that during his caravan trade journeys, Muhammad became acquainted with Christianityof the Monophysite Nestorian sects, "strongly influenced by the ascetic piety of monastic religion" (7). However, his contact with those Christians was social and personal rather than literal and religious.

Beginning from the prophetic life of Muhammad, the fundamental principles of Islam had been laid down in accord with both the Qur'anic injunctions and of the Semitic customs and traditions concerning almost all important aspects of Muslim life, especially the Fundamental Principles or The Five Pillars. Whatever action the Prophet did, they were akin to both Arab and Judeo-Christian modes.

The language of the Qur'an, for instance, is the old Arab poetical language, the rhymed prose. And the age-old Arab customs and practices (sunnah) absorbed by Islam, incorporated in the life of the Prophet Muhammad, came to be known "the prophetic Sunnah", (his tradition). When the Prophet and his followers (Muslims) migrated to Yathrab (later named madinat al-nabi, the city of the Prophet) in

622 C.E. Islam adopted the Arab lunar calendar which came to be known as the <u>Hijra</u> Calendar.

Socially, although Islam abolished the <u>traditional Arab tribal structure and founded the social system of equality, brotherhood, love, sharing and caring</u>; yet in Islam the Arab custom of individual naming continued. A person was known as the son of someone, for example, Muhammad <u>ibn</u> 'Abdullah ibn 'Abdul Muttalib ibn Hashim ibn 'Abdul Mannaf. (A person might also be called by a parenting name (<u>kunya</u>) as <u>abu/abi</u> or the <u>umm</u>= father or mother) of a son (not a daughter). By the way, sometimes even a deceased first born: for example, Muhammad was called <u>abu al-Qasim</u> (father of Qasim). There was a third kind of name which Islam has also used, namely, the <u>laqab</u> (nicknaming) which indicated some kind of special characteristic—sometime the birthplace or some special skill, e. g. Hakim <u>Madani</u> and Akbar <u>Qawwal</u>, respectively.

<u>Pre-islamic elements</u>: Islam has also continued <u>old Arabic names</u> like slave of a particular god or goddess such as, 'Abdullah (slave of Allah); one of the chief gods of southern Arabia, <u>allah</u>, Islam has adopted that name for its only One God.

Economically, Mecca, the birth place of the Prophet Muhammad, was a commercial city on the camel route in ancient times. In that city there was also a banking system as well as money lenders. Because of this commercial phenomenon, there was a gap between the very wealthy and the rest. As a result, there was a social tension created by the money-hunters—wealthy merchants. It is also well-known that young Muhammad <u>ibn</u> 'Abdullah and his contemporaries like Abu Bakr, 'Uthman and others belonged to that group of the society. Under those circumstances, Islam not only leveled the social structure, but also banned that notorious interest (<u>riba</u>); notwithstanding, Islam encourages the old Arab tradition of business (<u>bai' washera'</u>: Q. 2.

75f., 278ff; 3. 130). However, Islam maintains the old Arab tradition of trade and commerce.

Concerning the social-economic life, there were a few <u>concerns of pre-Islamic Arabia which Islam absorbed</u> in a manner that shows the continuation of the Arab legacy. "There is a set of complex arithmetical rules for dividing the property of a deceased person. Those appear to have been designed to ensure that all the close relatives of the male and female, is receive an appropriate share of what he leaves. Now this is very appropriate to the situation of the embryonic Islamic community"(8). Therefore, on the basis of that pre-Islamic system of inheritance, Islam has developed a complex system of inheritance (<u>mirath</u>) (9). In this matter, it appears that Islam has developed individualistic principles regarding all human matters—religious, ethical-moral, and social. As it is well-known, a Muslim, in the absence of a priesthood, is individually responsible for his/her deeds to Allah.

To end the social matters, <u>the polity set up by the Prophet</u> himself was similar to a federation of Arab tribes in accord with the pre-Islamic conceptions. However, it differed from such a federation not by its general structure, but only by certain decisions about policy. Muslims, being in the majority, the Prophet, whenever it was possible, admitted other tribes into the federation when they became Muslims.

In the sphere of religion, polytheism had been in a rapid decline, despite some opposition to the Prophet's preaching, and in the religion of nomads, which was a "tribal humanism", "there was also a widespread trend especially in important places like Mecca, towards a vague 'monotheism', with the expansion of Islam, that tendency was accelerated—and vague monotheism even outside the Islamic community, came more and more to resemble Qur'anic monotheism"(10). For example, the Ridda (Wars of Apostasy) had the same philosophy and technique comparable to those of the Islamic vision, even though the false prophets did not accept Islam. However, the complete life of Arabia in general did not change for some time, even though some aspects of it had been modified and transformed ingeniously.

Further, many Biblical names, as many as 27 are those of well-known prophets, names of many tribes are found in the Qur'an (11). Abraham's sunna (way) stands out as the model to be followed by the Muslims in some ways (Q. 2.124, 135f.; 23.95; 16.123); and some of the Biblical laws have been incorporated into the Islamic system in some form.

With the expansion of Islam to the Fertile Crescent (roughly the Near-East), inhabited by both non-Semitic and Semitic peoples, Islam, beginning in 636 C. E. conquered this whole area, and introduced Arabic as the lingua franca replacing Aramaic. Here, as in other places, Islam absorbed, mutatismutandis, the cultural elements of the former peoples. Referring to this area, Philip J. Stewart says, "Between the Semitic and the Arab-Islamic ages, this whole area had been under the control of three other peoples, the Persians, founders of the first large scale empire, the Sasanid, centered on Mesopotamia; the Greeks, who colonized the shores of the Mediterranean, especially the Hellenistic period under the Macedonian Alexander; and the Romans whose empire eventually came to include Syria, Persia and Egypt"(12). For example, the "Patriarch of the Hebrews", Abraham (Ar. Ibrahim) had two sons, namely, Ishmael (Ar. Isma'l), born of Hagar (cf. Bible Gen. ch.15), and Isaac (Ar. Ishaq), (cf. Gen. Ch. 17; Q. 14. 39), who became the ancestors of the Arabs and Hebrews respectively. The Qur'an tells the story of how Ibrahim and Isma'il settled in Mecca and rebuilt the ka'ba for the worship of One God (cf. Q.2. 125 ff.; 22. 26). Northern Arabia is traced back to Abraham through his son, Ishmael. Arabs are referred to ten times in the Bible (cf. Gen. 25.18). <u>Islamic Tradition mentions that Ibrahim, who left his Egyptian maid, Hagar, in the valley of Safa and Marwa near Mecca</u>, where she gave birth to her son, Isma'il, later visited Mecca where he, along with son Isma'il, rebuilt the ancient <u>ka'ba</u>, now the place of Muslim pilgrimage. Muslims find nearby the scene of the Biblical story of how God tested Abraham's faith by ordering him to sacrifice his son, Isma'il, and how, just as the knife was about to cut, He provided instead a ram caught in bushy plants (Gen. 22. 1-14). It should be mentioned here that Muslims are also required to believe in all the prophets without making any distinctions (Q.2. 285; 3. 84).

There are <u>two laws of the Pentateuch which have been integrated into Islamic law</u>. For example, there was a prohibition on the consumption of pig meat, and on the eating of meat containing surplus blood, which meant that animals must be slaughtered. "As regards economic life, there was a prohibition on lending at interest to fellow Jews, which did not apply to loans to non-Jews"(13). Islam, too, forbids lending at interest, but without any exception (Q. 2.275f.). A third regulation Islam has also adopted from the Jewish law is the circumcision of males, an Abrahamic <u>sunna</u> (14). Moreover, <u>there are other Jewish laws, such as "an eye for an eye and a tooth for a tooth</u>, (Ex. 21.24); the death sentence for capital crimes like fornication, adultery and rape (Deut. 22.21; 22.25); and other capital crimes (Deut. 17. 2-7), adopted by Islam in some forms"(15).

Islam has also developed the eschatological matters like the ancient Egyptian ideas, as stated in the <u>Book of the Dead</u>, such as the expectation of the end of the world; resurrection; the Day of Judgement (the Last Day); weighing of the worldly works; and finally, God's judgment considering the worldly deeds, and the final destination—heaven or hell (16).

The Qur'an also mentions Satan (17). According to the (2.34, 36; 7.11-18 et passim verses) Shaytan, originally one of the angels, named Iblis, disobeyed Allah's (God's) order to salute Adam, after He created him, from clay (tin), at which God cursed Iblis and expelled him from paradise. Since then, he, with Allah's permission though, is allowed to mislead and delude first Adam and Eve, then mankind all the way up to the Day of Judgement (18). At the same time, as Islam advanced through peace and war, the umma (community) rose with many new ideas, as discussed above, Islamic intellectuality began to play a new role in Muslim life. Some of those schools like the Mu'tazilites, 'Asharites, Kharijites, Murijites and Shi'aites, taking the advantage of Islamic liberalism, developed different divisions. They used Greek rationalism, widening further the boundary of Islamic intellectuality. Some Muslims developed an Islamic philosophy, mainly based on Greek philosophical ideas.

Likewise, on the spiritual level, Islam adopted Indian and Christian mystical ideas which resulted in the development of mysticism (Sufism) which played an important role in preaching and converting people to Islam, a role which opened the door for the percolation of non-Islamic ideas into Islam. Surprisingly, during those days of intellectual and spiritual development, there had never been any armed/philosophical clashes among those groups, because they communicated only through dialogue and each group respected the other's views.

Similarly, as Islam extended to the continents of Asia, Africa and to the West beyond Pyrenees into Spain and Sicily, more alien—Asian, African and European—newer ideas entered into the domain of Islam, especially through converts. The Muslim jurists (fuqaha) who exercised their tolerance and liberalism did not discard those non-Muslim ideas and elements unless they were completely incompatible with the Islamic system, kept, mutatismutandis.

Politically, with the disappearance of the unity of the Umma, as the Prophet himself established, some politically dissatisfied groups raised their heads in the community, and borrowing some theological ideas, especially from Christianity, formed separate religious-political groups such as the Shi'a Muslims. Notwithstanding their minority position, they have never been molested, let alone uprooted from the Muslim world until the present day. Here is an unparalleled example of Islamic liberalism and tolerance. In fact, Islamic liberalism integrated them not only as a theologically different group, but as an inseparable part of the Umma.

Looking at the other part of the Umma, Islamic political expansion outside the Arabian Peninsula required the codification of a new law, since the Qur'anic laws do not have enough provisions to administer a very large Muslim Empire. During the process of the formation or codification of this law (Shari'a), Muslim jurists (fuqaha) liberally used it, in addition to the Qur'an, hadith, or sunnah, consensus (ijma') and analogical deduction (qiyas).

The liberalism of the Shari'a can be praised for the fact that non-Muslim subjects have been given a special status (dhimmi, protected people) with complete assurance of freedom of religion, social right, freedom of movement with protection, only with the payment of protection fee (jizya) in lieu of military service. (More about the dhimmis will be discussed later).

In the area of peace and war, since the Prophet's time, the Muslims were faced with the situation of engaging in defensive wars against those who wanted to wipe out Islam in its bud. To face that situation, the Muslims, beginning from the Battle of Badr to the Battle of Tabuk fought 68 wars (gozwa and sariya), 16 of them (gozwa) commanded by the Prophet himself.

Modern age: Diplomatically, Muslims are not behind any other nations. For instance, during the Muslim Empire Age up to the fall of Baghdad in 1258, there were diplomatic missions from non-Muslim countries. However, beginning from the Ottoman (Turkish-Muslim) Empire, formal diplomatic mission exchanges with the non-Muslim countries were a common practice. Muslim nations today are members of all international organisations, and have diplomatic relations with almost all democratic nations of the world. Muslim nations follow an internationally recognised policy of "peace with all, malice with none" or "live in peace and let live in peace".

In the field of trade and commerce, present day Muslim nations follow the same practice of the ancient Arab traders with international trading practices. By the way, of the 16 OPPC countries, save Brazil, all are Muslim countries, and Saudi Arabia is the Number One oil producing country.

Finally, during this modern age, Islamic liberalism, hand-in-hand with modernism, ushered an age of unprecedented cooperation between the streams of ideas which resulted in an international cooperation between the Muslim world and the rest of the world, particularly the West. In this age, Muslim countries from Egypt and Turkey, all the way to Malaysia, Indonesia and the Sultanate of Brunei, have been modernised with complete cooperation with the rest of the world, especially with the West. "Muslims have learned to live comfortably and confidently in non-Muslim countries, including non-Semitic ones, as fully pledged citizens of those countries"(19).

During this age, there were some outstanding Muslim scholars and reformers, like Sayyid Ahmad Khan, Sayyid Amir 'Ali, Muhammad 'Abdullah, Rashid Reda, Shah Walyullah, to name only a few outstanding ones. These individuals and their companions played outstanding roles in the Muslim world of their times, using their varied personalities in both religious-cultural and political areas.

Thus, reflecting on the beginning and development of the Islamic civilization as a multi-dimensional way of life, yet changing throughout its history, as the circumstances demanded, Philip H. Stoddard says, "Islam, as a complete, complex civilization in which, ideally, individuals, societies and government must all reflect the will of God. In essence, it is a system of rules or laws to be followed in which the sacred is not separated from the secular" (20). "The rise of Islam", continues Stoddard, "not only brought empires into being, it also fostered the flowering of civilizations and the development of centres of learning, a melding of new thought with ancient ideas from East and West, took place, producing great contributions in medicine, physics, astronomy, geography, architecture, art, language, literature and history" (21). This knowledge—an amalgamation of the ancient Greco-Roman, Chinese-Indian, Arab-Muslim, and Persian-Turkic, kept alive, and promoted in course, academic centres, and libraries of the Muslim countries—was eventually passed, through trade and commerce, as well as diplomatic interaction, and academic and scientific exchange, to the city-states and kingdoms of the Iberian Peninsula and Italy, leading those Western Christian regions into the Renaissance before any other part of Europe." "At a time when the Dark Ages had Europe under its grip", continues the learned author, "the Muslim World shored with the light of knowledge and progress. The contribution made by Islam and Muslims to the Renaissance of Europe is the greatest gift Islam has bestowed upon that continent" (22).

CHAPTER 1 : References

1. Arnold, T.W., "Islam", <u>Shorter Encyclopaedia of Islam (SEI)</u>; also cf. Lidzbarski, "Islam and Salam", ZS, i., 85 sqq.; also cf. <u>Sura</u> 3.19: "The [true] religion with Allah is al-Islam", and 5.3: "This day have I perfected for you your religion and completed My favour towards you, and approved AL-ISLAM for you as a religion", p. 132.

2. Esposito, John L., <u>Islam: The Straight Path,</u> New York, Oxford University Press, 1988, pp. 3f.; also cf. De Boer, T. J., <u>The History of Philosophy in Islam</u>, tr. Edward R. Jones, Dover Publication Inc., New York, 1967, p. 7.

3. Smith, W. Robertson, <u>The Religion of the Semites: Their Fundamental Institutions</u>, Schocken Books, New York, 1972, p. 152.

4. Schoeps, Hans-Joachim, <u>The Religions of Mankind: Their Origin and Development</u> (translated from the German by Richard and Clara Winston), Anchor Books, Doubleday & Company, Inc., Garden City, New York, 1968, p. 187.

5. "Islam", <u>Shorter Encyclopaedia of Islam</u>.

6. Watt, W. W., <u>What is Islam</u>, Longmans Green and Company LTD., London, 1968, P. 3.

7. Schoeps, <u>op, cit.</u>, p. 243.

8. Watt, <u>op. cit.</u>, p. 110.

9. Cf. Q. 4. 11f. 19; Schacht, "Mirath", <u>SEI</u>.

10. Watt, <u>op. cit.</u>, pp. 111f.

11. Prophets of Allah mentioned in the Bible and the Qur'an (see ch. 2, v. 20).

12. Steward, P. J.,Unfolding Islam, 1st. ed., Ithaca Press, UK, 1994, p. X111.

13. Ibid., P. 7, ref. to Deut., 23, 19-20.

14. Gen., 7, 6-14.

15 .For retaliation, (Q. 2.178 f.; 5. 45); for adultery, (Q. 24. 2 f., 26); for idolatry, (Q. 4. 48, 52, 76, 116; 5. 639. 3, 5; 8.6, etc.).

16. Cf. Smith, op. cit., pp. 72, 272, 419f. Some suggest that from Persia (Iran) came the belief in eternal reward in Paradise (from Persian Pairidaiza, 'an enclosure of part') and eternal punishment in Hell (Gehinnam, the name of a smouldering rubbish dump, outside Jerusalem, as opposed to the Sheol of the Old Testament (cf. Stewart, op. cit., pp. 8f.)

17. Cf. A. J. Wensinck, "Iblis", SEI.

18. Stewart, op. cit., p. 9.

19. Hedayetullah, M., Dynamics of Islam: An Exposition, Trafford, 2002, Victoria, B. C., p. 31.

20. Change and the Muslim World, Syracuse University Press, Syracuse, 1981, P. 2.

21. Ibid., p. 8.

22. Hedayetullah, op. cit., p. 3.

CHAPTER 2

<u>The Life of the Prophet Muhammad</u>

To write about the Prophet Muhammad's life, we have to search for information, to begin with, in the Qur'an itself, then the <u>hadith</u> then in history books. It is said that "Muhammad himself was the great architect of Islam".

The Qur'an itself contains a good deal of authentic information about the Prophet himself. Apart from the Qur'anic information, historically it is known that Muhammad <u>ibn</u> 'Abdullah was born in 570 C. E. in a Qurashite family, and died in 632 (cf. Q. 'umr, <u>sura</u> 18.16). Since his mother died in his early age, the orphan Muhammad was brought up under the guardianship of his grandfather, 'Abdul Muttalib, then by his uncle, Abu Talib (cf. Q. <u>sura</u> xciii. 6f.). We are also told that his boyhood was a bit unlike that of common youngsters: he was not a playful, rather a thoughtful young man about something. However, as he grew up to the age of 25, his interest in business was apparent (cf. <u>sura</u> ii. 108; lxii. 9 sq); he is reported to have become a sort of business adviser to a widow named Khadija, who was fifteen years older than he (cf. F. Buhl, "<u>Khadidja</u>", <u>SEI</u>). Eventually, they got married and had a few children, but none of them reached the age of manhood. That is why the Qur'an says: "Muhammad is not the father of any man among you, but he was the messenger of Allah and the Seal of the Prophets; and Allah is Aware of all things"(33. 40; also cf. <u>Sura</u> 93). He is also known to have maintained a polygyny family even though he was not the father of man, as stated above. Nonetheless, he is also known as the "Father of Qasim" (<u>abul qasim</u>).

That means, Qasim died before reaching the age of manhood. This is a historical fact; still it is a matter of controversy as to how a person of that age became a successful adviser of a well-known business lady, irrespective of the age difference. Reflecting on this question, some said that at that early age to be a successful business man must have been caused by his early meditative life, that is to say, development of internal maturity. We are also told that he had been a "thoughtful boy rather than a playful boy". He did not play with his contemporaries, who were surprised for that manner. This was, for sure, a God-given talent for a young man to become the business adviser—partner of a well-known business lady. What a wonderful historical fact, considering the age difference. It goes without saying, Muhammad, an orphan (<u>yatim</u>), young man, needed a guardian and helper to proceed with his life, still uncertain of his future. His early meditative life is certainly an indication of his future life, as it did happen—a Prophet of Allah (God). (1).

In <u>suura</u> XC iii, we are told that Allah made the poor orphan prosperous. "God found thee wandering and guided thee (cf. <u>sura</u> Xlii: 52: "Thou did not know what book or belief was". He was neither a pagan nor schooled. (for his early life, in Mecca, sanctified place, he considered: cf. <u>sura</u> xxvii. 91; xxviii.57; xxix.67; cviii. 2; vii. 31f.).

It is reported that at about the age of 40, Muhammad began having vision. Tradition also reports that in his serious piety, he withdrew one night to Mount Hira, in the neighbourhood of Mecca, where the angel Gabrael appeared to him and asked him to read the contents of the <u>sura</u> 96: "Read, read in the name of Allah, and is known by the title "Congealed Blood". At dawn, the angel stood against the horizon, wherever Muhammad turned. Muhammad was very scared. He rushed home to his wife, Khadija, and asked her "wrap me up, wrap me up" because he was very cold. She called her uncle, Waraqa b. Nawfal, a Christian priest, who recognised that that was a divine revelation and Muhammad will be a Prophet. (sura 96) is the first revelation. The word ummi applied to him (Q. 7. 15) means no schooling. But a merchant he was. After his wife, the first believer was 'Ali. They convinced him that it was a divine messenger.

Nevertheless, he had to wait for a year or more before a new vision (wahy) gave him the assurance that he was indeed a rasul of Allah. The next event was the wahy telling "O wrapped one, stand up, yes, admonish your Lord, yes praise Him. Your clothes, yes, cleanse them. Be not kind out of selfishness. And your Lord, yes, wait for Him"(2). He was influenced particularly by Christian sects, later also by the Jews. Ideas from the caravans passing, also communication by sea with Abyssinia, and from foreign merchants visiting the great markets in Mecca. In addition, Christianity had established itself among many Beduin tribes, for example, Bakr, Hanifa, Taiy, while Jewish colonies were settled in Yathrab (later named Madina) and the oases north of it. Muhammad, living in Mecca, had many opportunities to come in contact with the Christians in particular. Christians also took part in the pilgrimage in Mecca. In the Qur'an, alongside Aramaic expressions many Ethiopic borrowed words are found showing religious influence from Abyssinia. According to Tore Andrae, Muhammad was very close to Christianity and even "dependent" on Christianity, which needs a great deal of research and investigation to establish this claim historically. "After calling attention to the wide dissemination and dominating position of Nestorianism in the Persian empire, which is of importance as it must have been much more accessible to Muhammad than Monophysitism; . . ." (3). It is further stated that it is remarkable in many respects that the Prophet's teaching is close to the teaching of the church, for instance, "in the account of the birth of Jesus and his miraculous gifts and in the undeniable echos of the doctrine of the Logos (sura iii. 39; iv. 171) (4). But during the Meccan period (e. g. sura xliii.57 sqq) Prophet Muhammad unequivocally rejected the belief that Jesus Christ was the son of God and unconditionally denied that he had ever asserted anything of that kind about himself.

We can conclude what we know from the Qur'an about the Prophet's knowledge is supplemented in a very important way by tradition, according to which he was not alone in his search for a purer religion. There were many people, like Muhammad, who were dissatisfied with the pagan Arab religion and tradition, and who were looking for a more reasonable and intellectual faith, especially a cousin of Khadija, Waraqa b. Nawfal. In addition, there were the Hanafis whose tradition is well-known in the history of the Arabs. To continue the history of Muhammad's pre-prophetic life, we are told that "While Muhammad was in a state of great spiritual excitement as a result of contact with the religious ideas that penetrated into Arabia, something happened which suddenly transformed his whole consciousness and filled him with a spiritual strength which decided the whole course of his life: he felt himself called to proclaim to his countrymen as a prophet the revelations which were communicated to him in a mysterious way"(5).

The Qur'an gives some hints about the manner of the inspirations before receiving revelations; a veil lay over them which the Prophet could not raise completely. Most probably the wrapping up (1xxiii.1; 1xxiv.1) refers to a preparation for receiving of the wahy in the manner of Arab kahin. We reject the gossip or malicious talks of those who say that Muhammad was possessed (majnun), a soothsayer (kahin), a magician (sahir), for they show that during his times of wahy, he made a sort of impression close to those figures, mentioned above, widely known in pre-Islamic or ancient Arabia. In fact, there are several hadith (traditions) which describe his condition in such moments more fully and are accepted as genuine, for those mysterious seizures provided to those accused him the most valid evidence for the divine origin of his inspiration. "From the scientific point of view the fact is that the voice heard by him only uttered what he had from time to time heard from others and which now cropped up out of his subconscious". "The scientific student", continues the learned author, "therefore does see Muhammad a deceiver but fully agrees with the impression of sincerity and truthfulness which his utterances in the older revelations make" (6). The historical facts were that he honestly went through years of hostility and even "humiliation in Mecca in the unshakable conviction of his lofty task" (7).

With the help of the Qur'an and <u>Hadith</u>, it is possible to get a satisfactory clear idea of the Prophet's condition when revelations came to him. The fundamental idea in it is the fact that a divine book existing in the heaven, <u>al-kitab</u>, a well-guarded book, which only the pure may touch (lvi. 79), a well-guarded tablet (lxxx. 21 sq.) the mother of the book (xliii. 3 sqq.), on honourable leaves, exalted and pure, by the hands of noble and pious scribes (lxxx.13, sq). It was revealed to him orally piece by piece in Arabic intelligible to him and to his countrymen (cf. xii. 1; xiii. 37; xx. 113; xxvl. 192 sqq; xii. 3; xliv. 58) and particularly xii. 44: "If We had made it a Qur'an in a foreign tongue, they would say: Why are its <u>ayat</u> ["signs, from the small sections of the text] not expounded intelligibly?, a foreign text and an Arab reader!"]. He received the revelations orally; Allah revealed to him the substance of the separate sections (lxxv. 16 sqq.), while in several passages it is stated clearly that the revelations were communicated through a Spirit (xxvi. 192 sq; xvi. 102; xlii. 52) or the Angel (xvi. 2; xv. 8; also cf. liii. 5 sqq.; lxxxi. 23sqq.); and a late <u>sura</u> of the Madina period (ii. 97) is precise to say that the revelations were sent through angel Gabrial. There were other events like his night journey revealed to him (cf. <u>sura</u> viii. 43; xvliii.

27; and liii. 10; lxxxi. 19). "These communications were the great miracle that was granted him, while he expressly and repeatedly says that the ability to perform miracle in the usual sense was denied to him (unlike Jesus)"(8).

Some of the ideas are based not on the dogmatic conception of monotheism but on the general religious and moral impression of which contact with older religions had made upon him, which eventually resulted in his break with polytheism. Specially, his mind was filled with the idea of the moral responsibility of man created by Allah, and with the idea of the judgement to take place on the day of resurrection, which points to Semitic belief. To this are added clear descriptions of the punishment of the hell-goers, and pleasant or reductive pictures of the happiness of paradise. Slowly, but surely, monotheism was emphasised as an overwhelming basic idea, and at the same time his conception of the nature of Allah was surely widening in accord with the Semitic tradition. Thus, with all the force of an elemental religious nature, he pointed to the wonderful aspects or matters of everyday life, especially to the wonderful phenomena of the every day life of man. The religious duties or obligations which were being imposed by Allah on him and his followers (Muslims) are simple and sparse. For example, briefly: belief in Allah, appeal to Him for forgiveness of sins (xxiii. 1-11), offer prayers frequently—finally 5 times a day and night (xi. 114; lxxiii. 20; also cf. lxxvi. 25 2q.), assist one's fellow-men, especially those who are in need; free oneself from the love of "delusive" wealth and from all forms of cheating (xxvi. 182 sq.; lv. 9 sq.) (important moral teaching for Mecca, in particular, an important commercial city; lead a chaste life and do not expose new-born girls as was the pre-Islamic barbarous Arab custom (cf. sura vi. 151; xvii. 31 from poverty). "This is the ideal of the truly pious man who is called by the name of muslim (lxviil. 35; xxi. 108) or hanif (x. 105f; xxx. 30; xcviii. 4; also cf. vi. 79).

From all these, it is fairly evident that Muhammad considered himself to be a "warner" (ii. 50; lxxiv. 2; lxxix. 45; lxxx. 11; lxxxviii. 21 sq.) in view of the coming of the Day of Judgment, to his fellow-Arabs, to whom no prophet had been sent until that time (vi.157; xxviii.46; xxxii. 3; xxxiv. 44 and xxxvi. 6). And as a result of the revelations, Allah has given a complete book of revelations, the Qur'an. The Jews and Christians must, therefore, testify to the truth of his mission and preaching (x. 94; xvi. 43; xxi. 7; xxvi. 197 and xxviii. 52).

Here we consider briefly how the Prophet's relations developed following his position as a Prophet: Considering all information from different sources such as Tabari, i. 1180 sq., 1224 sq, at first the Prophet met with no serious opposition, and in many cases his preaching was not rejected or protested against. In fact, in the words addressed to Salih (xi. 62) we may find an idea that he had at the beginning raised enormous expectations among his neighbours (Meccans). In fact, many people, including his wife, Khadija, Ali, Abu Bakr and many others accepted Islam (cf. "Muhammad", SEI, p. 395). By the way, they were all young people and thus not influential in the then Meccan society. However, when the full consequences of his ideas became clear, he attacked the religion of his society. When they realised that a religious revolution might endanger their faith, thus their fairs and their trade undoubtedly, that was the main cause of their attitude to the Prophet is clear from the fact that very often he tried to calm the fears of the Qurayesh on this point: the Meccan sanctuary, he emphasised, belonged to his God Allah, whom the Meccans also recognised as the highest God (xxxi. 25; xxix. 35; also cf. Qais b. al-Khatim, ed. Kowaleki. V. 14; xiii. 12 where Allah is the lord of the Ka'ba) and will protect and bless his sanctuary, if they submit to him (xxvii. 91; xxviii, 57; xxix. 67 etc). In addition, there was the conservative mentality of these businessmen in the field of religion and their opposition to or dislike of new ideas, especially to that of the resurrection of the dead to face judgement.

History records the inhuman persecution which the Prophet's followers suffered at the hands of the Meccans. There were inhuman persecutions of the followers of the Prophet (Muslims) which twice compelled the Muslims to migrate to Abysinia, and in the Qur'an there is mention of "trials" "which their opponents inflicted upon the believers, men and women (1xxxv. 10), and it is expressly mentioned that the influential wished to prevent Muhammad from praying (xcvi. 9 sq.; cf. the veiled account vii. 86). (10). Notwithstanding the above-mentioned historical facts, Prophet Muhammad's strength lay in the consciousness that he lived in a higher intellectual world (religious-moral) which was not available to the Meccans and that he proclaimed ideas "the equal of which neither men nor jinn with combined efforts could produce" (Q. xvii. 88). His most emphatical arguments in support of his mission rebounded from his opponents who were behind the wall of prejudices and arrogance, rather than rational and logical points of view, but based on material interest. Those circumstances eventually influenced the matter of his preaching in a remarkable way. For example, when his opponents mocked him because the divine judgment threatened by him did not happen (xxxviii. 16; 1xx. 5), he reminded them the earlier prophets had met extreme hostility and had, therefore, brought on themselves severe punishments. By the way, we are aware of the fact that at the beginning Prophet Muhammad's preaching had been sober, peaceful, and thus gave no offence to his hearers, particularly the oldest. It was undoubtedly the hardness of heart of his countrymen which compelled him to take this weapon in order to silence. To the Prophet, this resistance to the unquestionable truth was something so irrational that he could only find comfort in an idea which was to be of far-reaching importance in the further development at Islamic dogma or dogmatism: "Allah, the immeasurably exalted and almighty, could of course not be impeded by the resistance of mortals; the unbelief of the Prophet's opponents was therefore an effect of the divine will: "Allah makes to hear whom he [sic] will" (x.99; xxxii. 12 sqq.; xxxv. 8; lxxiv. 34 etc). By and large, despite the above-mentioned situation (also cf. xvi. 35; xxxvi. 47; xvi. 47 sq.), Prophet Muhammad's followers were not safe, which resulted in some of their migration to Abyssinia (Ethiopia), in order to maintain their new faith, Islam, safely. However, according to 'Urwa, some of those new Muslims gradually drifted back under those difficult conditions. It is also reported that in order to calm down the situation, the Prophet showed his soft heart, considering the difficult situation, declaring that the old Meccan gods, Lat, Monat and 'Uzzat might be regarded as "divine beings whose intercession was effectual with Allah. This led to a general reconciliation news of which reached Abyssinia and indeed a number of the Muslims there to return home"(11). However, not too long after that, the situation changed because the agreement had been for a short period of time, since the Prophet had quickly realised those words as "interpolations of satan" and had substituted for them the words which we now have in sura iii. 19-23.

It should be mentioned emphatically that during his struggling life in Mecca under those circumstances, mentioned above, his success was possible only with the support of the members of his family, save Abu Lahab who on this account is perpetually condemned in the Qur'an (sura cx1) along with his wife, who boldly fulfilled their duty in this matter.

During the last phase of the Prophet's Meccan life, there was the famed nocturnal journey (isra'/mi'raj) later so celebrated, to the "remotest place of prayer" to which xvii. 1 briefly refers. Some say it was a vision, which made on him an impression of a real journey to heaven (where he met Allah from behind thousands of screens—some say 70,000) (12). According to the widely held opinion, the end of this journey was the temple in Jerusalem, and conclusions are drawn from this event about the significance which this city then had for him. However, some writers like Horovitz (ibid., ix. 159 sqq.) have tried to show that al-masdjid al-aksa refers to the place of prayer of the angels in heaven (cf. vii. 206; xxvix. 175), for which view many reasonable arguments can be given, especially that the nocturnal journey is associated with the journey to heaven as early as in the tradition given by Ibn Ishaq, and that in the Qur'an there are several times a reference to an ascent into heaven (vi. 35; xvii. 95; xv. 14 sq.).

One of the important elements of his teaching was the rejection of the Christological dogmas of the church. This is certainly from the conversation with his pagan opponents (Q. x1iii. 57 sqq) during his life in Mecca. This, of course, did not affect his idea of the basic of Islam with the older Semitic revelation, but only the wrong doctrine later adopted in the church, for he knew that Jesus vigorously rejected his divinity.

His position in Mecca had not been safe and secure, especially after the death of Khadija and Abu Talib. After their death, his position in Mecca became more and more dangerous or peculiarly unsafe. An attempt to establish himself in Taif brought him into serious danger, thus the question of safety became a serious matter. Notwithstanding that situation, the Prophet stood firm in his mission with belief in Allah's protection. In fact, he was determined to perform his mission as a "warner and could regard it as the will of Allah that his countrymen were not to be saved (cf. Q. x. 99; x1iii. 89). Reflecting on that unpleasant situation, one author says, "But the consciousness of being a chosen instrument of Allah, had gradually became so powerful within him that he was no longer able to sink back into an inglorious existence with his object unachieved" (13).

The same author continuous to say more words forcefully. Thus he says, "His astonishing gift of being able to exert a powerful religious suggestion even on men who were intellectually superior to him, imperiously demanded a wider sphere of activity than a small number of adherents, mostly without influence" (14). In addition to what is stated above, there was a factor, namely, his mental exhaustion and his lack of new ideas. Under those circumstances, he was thinking of going to some other place outside Mecca, irrespective of difficulties for an Arab (himself) to break the links that bound him to his family and tribe.

The gathering of the people from all parts of the country for the pilgrimage gave the Prophet an opportunity to meet some people from Yathrab (later named Madina—City of the Prophet after his migration there). The pilgrims from Yathrab met the Prophet more than once and assured him of their help and cooperation in preaching his mission (Islam). The Jewish population of that city is known to have prepared the ground for preaching there a branch of Semitic religion, Islam.

The ground appeared to be ready for the Prophet's hijrat (migration) to Yathrab. In consideration of the two different situations in two cities, God blessed his Prophet, Muhammad, with generous idea to live and promote his mission of prophethood in two totally different social environments. Commenting on this new social-religious environment, in Yathrab, one writer says: "With this we are faced with one of the most difficult problems in the biography of Muhammad, the double personality which he presents to us". "The inspired religious enthusiast, whose ideas mainly centered around the coming last judgment, who had borne all insults and attacks, who only timidly touched on the possibility of active resistance (Q. xvi. 126) and preferred to leave everything to Allah's intervention, with the migration to Madina enters upon a secular stage and at one stroke shows himself a brilliant political genius"(15). It is suggested that the Prophet's eye in Mecca look in the wider social-political situation is evident from the prophecy in sura xxx. 2 sqq. Keeping in mind the background of his followers' migration to Abyssinia and his compromise with the polytheists in Mecca, we have evidence in him of a personality. This background tells us that the Madinese would certainly not have thought of finding in him a saviour from their social-political chaos and disorders if they had not found in him the abilities to resolve them.

The Madinese, it should be mentioned here, who had met the Prophet in al-Aqaba on the occasion of the hajj, as mentioned before, began spreading Islam in their land along with men whom the Prophet sent there to prepare the ground for his hijra (migration) in 622 C. E. It should also be stated here clearly that the Madinese who had met the Prophet at al-Aqaba over three consecutive years had pledged a 'formal agreement' in the name of their fellow citizens to take him into their community and to protect him as one of their own fellows, which was also good for his Meccan followers if they came to Yathrab. However, in this connection, tradition mentions only the promise of the Madinise to take Muhammad under their protection and not his followers. Notwithstanding, without some protection from some people, his followers could not have gone to Yathrab. Meccan Muslims slipped away in large or small numbers, so that eventually the Prophet along with Abu Bakr, leaving 'Ali behind, could go away safely, which they did. Traditions also confirmed by sura ix. 40 where it is mentioned that the Prophet along with his companion (Abu Bakr) stopping or hiding in the cave. The Migration (hijra) of The Prophet (cf. Carra de Vaux, SEI).

The migration of the Prophet (the hijra), taken by the Muslims as the beginning of their calendar or chronology for it constitutes the first stage in a movement which in a short period of time became of importance in the history of the world. According to the normal calculation, the Prophet arrived in Quba' a suburb of Yathrab, on the 12th Rabi' 1 of the first year, i. e., Sept. 24, 622 C. E. and immediately after went into his new home.

The tasks which he had to perform put the greatest strain on his diplomatic capacity. His companions (sahaba) were the only ones on whom he could depend. In addition, of course, there were those Madinese who had already adopted Islam, the ansars (helpers). He found open opposition from the Aws Allah; and a small number who, while did not oppose the Prophet openly, only reluctantly accepted the new religion, the traitors (munafiqun), who caused him continuous anxiety. Their leader was Khazraji 'Abdullah b. Ubaiy, "who possessed the munafiq quality of irresolution to such an extent that he regularly let slip every occasion on which he might have offered successful opposition" (16). The bitter feud between Aws and Khazraj was also a cause of a problem for the Prophet and his mission. Finally, there were the Jewish tribes (Banu Nadir, Banu Quraiza, Banu Qainuqa and the judaicised tribes in Madina"), they were the rich farmer groups, and unlike the Arab tribes, were prosperous. Their wealth and the support they had in the Jewish colonies in Khaibar, in particular, were to the Prophet's advantage. They would support or champion the truth of his preaching. His relations with the Christians in Madina were no longer totally unstrained, since he had begun even during his life in Mecca to reject the Christian "Orthodox ecclesiastical Christology". Nevertheless, he had greater sympathy with them than with the former (Jews). (cf. Q. v. 82; 1vii. 27).

Next, the Prophet had to find the ways and the means to form a united Community of the Muslims in Madina. There was another problem there: how to settle the Muslim emigrants or refugees from Mecca to procure the necessary means of substance? "To strengthen their claims for protection, he ordered the relationship of brotherhood to be created between each emigrant [mohajir] and a man of Madina [ansar] (17).(Ibid.). This arrangement, plus the brotherhood between every two mahajir, was abolished after the battle of Badar in 624 C. E. (cf. sura xxxiii. 6). On the other hand, when the Prophet's relations with the Jews had begun to be strained or bitter, an important diplomatic gift began to emerge, the ideal for it allowed him to use it for constituting an umma, fundamentally for practical considerations. It is a matter of fact that the highest authority is Allah and the Prophet, before whom all important matters are laid; but the umma included also some Jews and pagans, so that the legal forms of the traditional Arab tribes are considerably preserved. However, it was soon rendered obsolete by the quick change of the conditions.

It is a proof of the Prophet's political diplomacy that he tried to attach Jews to himself by taking over a few features of their worship. For example, he made the 10th Muharram a day of fasting, obviously following the Jewish fast on the 10th Tishri, the Day of Atonement. Some say Muslim midday prayer (zuhar) probably is based on Jewish practice (cf. ba'uta, ii. 230), and the easier rule about purification before the obligatory salat (iv. 43; v. 96). On the other hand, the introduction of the Friday congregational prayer might have also been Jewish Friday prayer. Finally, whether the choice of Jerusalem as qibla for Muslim ritual prayer is also following Jewish tradition is controversial (18). Notwithstanding all the concessions the Prophet made to the Jews, the relationship with them did not improve. The Prophet might have miscalculated his relations with them. They were expecting the coming of the Messiah, and since Prophet Muhammad was not that, they did not show any interest in having any relations with him. As a result, only a small number of Jews recognised him as a Prophet (Q. iii. 110). Anyway, the Prophet's relation with the Jewish people was finally settled by the revelation of the Qur'anic vs. 4. 44; 3.119, and even this, included a number of special laws adapted to the particular age (4. 160; 6. 146; xvi. 118) but they(Jews) had also put away all sorts of things in their holy scriptures (2. 42, 146, 159, 174; 3. 77) and indeed had even falsified their scriptures (2. 59; 4. 46; 5. 13, 47; 7. 162). By the way, the Jews were not able to deny these assertions.

Having finished his religious controversy with both Jews and Christians, he felt himself called upon to reform the deteriorated religions of revelation, each of which confirmed it was the only true one (Q. 2. 113). "As a result, he now claimed a special place among the prophets: he is seal of the prophets (33. 40), to whom Jesus himself had pointed by the name Ahmad (lxi. 6; also cf. 3. 87). But, nonetheless, the early years after the migration to Medina, constituted the period when Islam was born as an independent religion for parallel with his opponents' criticisms of the religions of revelation, and in particular opposition to Judaism ran a positive shopping of Islam.

Islam as a national religion has maintained some elements of the old Arab culture and absorbed them into Islam mutatis mutandis. In the second year of the hijra (July, 623-June, 624), after some thinking, he ordered that Jerusalem should not be the qibla at prayer any longer, instead the sanctuary of the Black Stone at Mecca (Q.2. 142-150) because it is a "gathering place and a safe retreat for men" (Q. 2. 125). His native city Mecca was made the centre of the Islamic religion, and the hajj to Mecca was constituted as one of the fundamental obligations for the rich Muslims, only once in life though (Q. 3. 96 sq.). By the way, Friday remains a significant week-day for congregational prayer for the Muslim community, but it was not to be a day of rest like the Jewish Sabbath (Q. lxii. 9 sq). Next, in place of the fasting on 'Ashura', Allah substituted the fasting from dawn to dusk in the month of Ramadan, the month in which he received the fundamental revelation (Q. 2. 185).

Commenting on the nature of Islam as an Arab national religion, Buhl says, "This nationalisation of Islam, which was to have so many results, gave Muhammad a final legitimation, which brought it into harmony with his earlier appeal to the religions of revelation, as he came forward as the restorer of the religion of Abraham (millat-i-Ibrahim), which had been corrupted by the Jews and Christians" (cf. "Muhammad", SEI). Abraham's son, Ishmael, the ancestor of the Arabs, founded the Ka'ba (the Meccan sanctuary) and the rites celebrated there, corrupted by the heathen, restored by the Prophet Muhammad (Q. 2. 124 sq.; 22. 26 sqq.).

While his religion, Islam, was being transformed from what is stated above, the Prophet's personal position was being slowly transformed by the changed situation. According to the programme or rules of the community, all important matters were to be laid before Allah and himself (cf. 3. 132, 172; 4. 13 sq., 59). From now on, alongside of the belief in Allah, now appears a belief in the Prophet (xlviii. 9; lxiv. 8). Allah is his protector, and the angels are at his disposal (lxvi. 4).

The elevation of Mecca to be the center of his religion imposed on the Prophet new tasks which were to lead to unexpected consequences. "If visiting the holy places in and around Mecca was a duty of the Muslims, who were excluded from the town (Q. 22. 25 sq.), the result was the inevitable necessity of forcing admission to them" (19). In addition, the Prophet had another case to settle with the Meccans who drove him out of his motherland. This situation led to a new command, that of the holy war (al-jihad)—war on the path of Allah). There were considerable difficulties in achieving this object. The Madinese pledged themselves to defend him, as one of their own only if he were attacked. The <u>muhajirun</u> (emigrants) were not ready for any warfare; nonetheless, they had to come out to fight along with their Prophet when the time came (Q. 2. 216; 22. 38 sqq.). He, however, succeeded in finding a way out of the difficulty which might be able to pave the way for military actions. After he sent different small armed forces which did not succeed in encountering the enemy, in the month of Rajab, the month in which all fighting was forbidden. Later, they succeeded in falling upon the caravan which felt secure until the end of the month, and one of the Meccans was killed. The rich plunder was sent to Madina, where in the meantime a storm of humiliation had broken out. The Prophet, however, gave the people time to recover and finally silenced them by the revelation of the <u>sura</u> 2. 217. The success of his policy had such an effect in Madina that not only emigrants buy also a good number of <u>ansars</u> offered their services, which he appealed for followers in Ramadan 2 A. H. in a new raid, which he himself commanded. At that time a rich caravan was coming from Syria, and the Muslims ambushed it at Badr. The Meccan caravan changed the normal route to escape the Muslim army but faced them at Badr. At the battle of Badr, a Muslim army of 315 under the command of the Prophet met the Meccan army of more than a thousand in battle and the Prophet won his first military victory against his own people from Mecca (cf. Q. 8. 5 sqq). The Prophet saw in this military encounter the wonderful help of the Almighty, who wished to force them to a war and He inspired His Prophet to fight the war which resulted in complete defeat of the superior enemy. Several Meccans were killed on the battlefield, and some of them, including the Prophet's uncle, Abbas, were brought as prisoners to Madina, where some of them were put to death, while others were held on ransom. This was a most important victory in the history of Islam, for the Prophet saw in the victory a powerful confirmation of his belief in the superiority of Allah (cf. Q. 8. 17, 65, iii. 123) and his own call, and, in addition, the commercial city of Mecca enjoyed such great prestige in Arabia that its conqueror was bound to attract all eyes to himself.

It should also be mentioned here that the victory at Badr added a new chapter to the Prophet's career; in addition to being a family man, a messenger of God, and a military commander. Beginning from this battle, the Muslims fought altogether 68 military conflicts—16 gozwa, commanded by the Prophet himself and 52 sarya commanded by his assistant commander. At Badr, he displayed a greater energy and ability to utilise the advantages he won. After he had drawn up the programme given in sura 8. 55 sqq., he besieged the Jewish tribe of Qainuqa'. The munafiqun, did not dare to oppose him, while the other Jews left their co-religionists in the middle of the difficulties (cf. Q. lix. 14) so that the latter were forced to migrate to Transjordania.

We also know that in order to protect himself while on the battlefield, the Prophet at that time adopted a plan which is further proof of his being an extraordinary political as well as military genius. He concluded, as shown from a few letters preserved as "lord of Madina, alliances with a number of Beduin tribes in which the two parties pledged themselves to assist one another"(20).

In the year 3 H./624-5, the Prophet continued his attacks on the Meccan caravans so that the Qurayesh finally realised the need for taking stronger measures to avenge their loss at Badr. An army of 3,000 men was equipped and marched towards Madina under the commandship of Abu Sufyan. The Prophet, instead of defending his city, Madina, marched out with his forces, which was reduced in number, thus in strength, because the munafiqun left the rank and of the Prophet's army, and took position at the foot of the hill of Uhud. Notwithstanding Meccan military superiority, the fighting at the beginning was in favour of the Muslims, until a number of archers, who had been placed in defending the Prophet, joined the battle against his orders, to grab rich booty, which enabled Khalid b. al-Walid to fall upon the Prophet's flank. As a result, many of the Muslims began to flee, particularly when the rumour spread that the Prophet had been killed (cf. Q. iii. 144). In reality, he was slightly wounded and escaped along with a few followers on the south side of the hill. The Meccans thinking that they had avenged their loss at Badr, quietly left for Mecca. It was a moment of sorrow for the Prophet and his followers, especially for the death of Hamza. Notwithstanding a setback at Uhud, the Prophet endeavoured to raise the morale of his followers by admonishment and censure alike. (cf. Q. 3. 118 sq., 139-160, 165-200). And the Prophet was not to stay quiet: The Jews, who had not taken part in the war, were happy to see the Prophet's misfortune, and several Bedouin tribes next year, had shown their attitude to him in an unfriendly way. It was, therefore, all the more necessary to set an example for others; and another Jewish tribe in Madina, the Banu Nadir, appeared to be a suitable object after Ka'b b. Ashraf 's murder had served as a prelude. It is made a charge against them in sura lix. 4, saying that they defy Allah and His messenger, on which account Tradition lays many crimes to them. After a siege of a few weeks, they (Banu Nadir) were forced to migrate to Khaibar or Syria. The Prophet distributed their left-over weapons and riches as booty (Q. lix. 6 sqq.).

Following the above-mentioned events, there came the revelation prohibiting the drinking of wine or intoxicating drinks in Islam (Q. 5. 90 sq.; also cf. lxxxiii. 25; xvi. 67; iv. 43; 2. 219). Drinking and gambling, the pre-Islamic Arab practices, were forbidden as games.

While the Prophet was trying to restore his "weakened authority", following the battle of Uhud, and a new threatening event came upon him. The Qurayesh, whose caravans were being regularly intercepted by the Prophet's army, and who were urged on by the

Jews of Khayber, recognised that the victory at Uhud had only been a blow in the air and realised the necessity of occupying Madina. They, along with some Beduin tribes, raised an army of about 10, 00000 men in the years 5/626-27), advanced to the siege Madina (cf. Q. 2. 429 sqq.). The siege of Madina by the Meccan army put enormous stress on the Prophet and his followers in Madina (cf. Q. 33. 10 sqq., 26). The Prophet, in order to strengthen the defense of the city, defended the city by digging ditches (khandaq, a Persian technique), in front of the unprotected areas of the city. The siege of the city dragged on for some time eventually under several circumstances, including the weather conditions, and forced the Meccan army to withdraw without any success. "For one section of the participants, however, the comedy of the war of the Ditch, was to become a bloody tragedy" (SEI). Hardly had the Meccan besiegers retired, than the Prophet declared war on the last Jewish tribes, the Banu Quraiza, and began to besiege their people of the town. After a long negotiation for peaceful settlement of the dispute, the Prophet accepted their surrender.

Despite the above-mentioned relations with the Jews, the problem of Jewish existence was not over yet; the Prophet organised the umma (Muslim Community) on a purely religious basis, which hitherto had been in the background for political reasons. On the other hand, he continued his attack on the Meccan caravans beyond the year 6/627-8, by and large punitive expeditions, on Bedouin tribes; of these expeditions, one important was against the Banu Mustaliq, which took place around this time, which created a serious conflict between the muhajirun and the ansar, and involved Prophet's wife, 'A'isha, in the celebrated adventure which almost cost her position as the wife of the Prophet, thus, mother-i-millat (mother of the Muslim umma) until a revelation saved her position (Q. 24. 4 sq., 11-20).

Towards the end of the year 6, the Prophet thought of his position so firmly established that he could try an expedition-military, of course, which would bring him close to his desired goal—the Mecca. He and his followers were still forbidden to go to Mecca and its holy places. However, through confidential agents, including his uncle, 'Abbas, he knew that feeling in the town had been gradually turning in his favour (cf. Q. xlviii. 15; ix. 7). On the other hand, an increasing number of Meccans being tired of endless and hopeless wars, thought it would be better for the commerce of Mecca to make a peace with their "indefatigable enemy" especially after he adapted into his programme the pilgrimages to their fairs, the sources of the city's wealth. Trusting to this revulsion of feeling, he asked his followers in Jul—Qa'da of the year 6 A. H./March, 628 to provide themselves with sacrificial animals and undertake an 'Umra with him to Mecca, as Allah in a vision had promised him a successful fulfillment of the visit (Q. xlviii. 27; also cf. 22. 29, 33). In consideration of his hostile relation, he probably wanted to perform a 'umra and stay there for a year until the next hajj (cf. Q. 2. 196 which probably belongs to this connection). The journey was, nevertheless, a risky one, so that he asked a few Beduin tribes to accompany him just in case they met with resistance. To his disappointment, however, they refused (Q. xlviii. 11 sq.) so that he decided to abandon the military nature of the march and asked his followers to go as harmless pilgrims. In Mecca, many were inclined to meet his wishes but the hostile party was still strong enough to get an army strong enough to meet him to prevent him from entering the town. He, therefore, encamped at al-Hudaibiya, where he began to negotiate with the Meccans through 'Uthman, who was protected by his family connection. But when the Meccans showed no signs of returning, on the one hand, and there was a rumour that he had been killed, on the other hand. At that time, the Prophet dropped all negotiations, and called his followers under a tree, probably a sacred one, and asked them to swear to fight for him or for Islam to the last, which they did with enthusiasm (Q. xlviii. 10, 18). But soon after, a few Meccan representatives arrived and offered a compromise by which he was to return this time, but to be allowed to perform an 'umra next year. He agreed to the compromise, concluded a ten years' truce with the Qurayesh, and also promised to surrender all Meccans of dependent status who came to the Prophet. However, his followers were not very happy; but the Prophet calmly ordered the sacrificial animals brought with them to be slain, which was to have been done at an umra in the town, and had his hair cut and bid his dissatisfied followers to do the same. "Only later did they discover that he had made a brilliant stroke of policy for he had included the Meccans recognise the despised fugitives and opponents of equal rank, and had concluded a peace with them which promised well for the future" (21).

He and his followers received plenty of compensation for the frustrated 'umra at the beginning of the year 7/628-9 by the capture of the fertile oasis at Khaibar which was the homeland of the Jews. It was the first conquest by the Prophet, and he instituted on this occasion a practice which subsequently became regular whenever Jews or Christians were captured: he did not put them to death nor banish them but let them remain on their lands as jimmis (tenants) with the payment of kharaj (land tax) annually. By the way, this expedition, which brought the Jewish colonies of Wadi'l-Qura into his power, made the Muslims wealthy (xlviii. 18-21).

Following the above-mentioned event, the Prophet sent letters to Muqawqis, governor of Alexandria; the ruler of Abyssinia, the Byzantine emperor and the Persian Shah (king), asking them to accept Islam. However, historians like Zaidan, in Hilal, 1904, p. 103 sq; JA, 1854, pp. 482 ff., do not think this letter was genuine. They argue that at a time when the Prophet was looking forward to conquer Mecca, the ultimate goal of his preaching a new religion, Islam, would indulge in writing letters to those monarchs, as mentioned above. It is very doubtful, contends the opposite side, if the Prophet Muhammad ever thought at all of his religion as a universal religion of the world (22). The passages in the Meccan <u>suras</u> which can be quoted in favour of this theory are (6. 90; 12. 104; 21. 107, 251; 34. 28; 36. 70; 38. 87, etc.). Besides, during the Madina period, the place of persuation and proof ("no compulsion in religion": 2. 256; also cf. 16. 125). The final consideration of the Prophet's decision after the agreement at Uhud—at the height of his power never demanded from Jews or Christians that they should accept Islam but was content with political subjection and the payment of <u>jizya</u>. Therefore, the real principle of the Prophet was to have a peaceful agreement with the non-Muslims to live in peace, rather than uprooting everyone on his way. For example, consider his dealing with the friendly Muqawqis (cf. Butler, <u>The Arab Conquest of Egypt</u>, 1902) and to assume that the idea of missionary enterprise arose only later under the influence of Christian tradition.

Later when the Prophet's position improved and was consolidated, he no longer asked for political agreement; instead, he demanded straightforward acceptance of his religion (Islam) which involved the five fundamental requirements.

In March 629 C. E., the Prophet performed the 'umra, as agreed upon by the peace treaty of Hudaibiya. Commenting on this event, one author says, "For him who had been driven out of his native city, it was undoubtedly a great satisfaction to be able to visit Mecca as the acknowledged lord of Madina; . . ." (Buhl, op. cit., p. 402). In the meantime, he continued his military efforts. His army suffered a setback in the first serious effort to extend his authority over the Arabs on Byzantine land, at Mu'ta in Trans-Jordan. Notwithstanding, several Bedouin tribes there considered the advantages they would get not only in this world but also in the after-world. A large group of Beduins like the Sulaim voluntarily adopted Islam and placed themselves under its flag of authority.

Notwithstanding the above situation, it was not comfortable for the Prophet that the heathens of his birthplace were preventing him from going to his homeland, Mecca (Q. 9. 12 sq.). Consequently, in Ramadan 8/629 he set out at the head of an army composed of muhajirin, ansar and Beduin. The news resulted in chaos and anxiety in Mecca, where the people who were supposed to fight to defend the city, slowly moved back, so that the more sensible new force could take over the control. Abu Sufyan, along with others, including the "Khuza'I Budail b. Waraqa, a friend of the Prophet, met him near the town, paid homage to him and obtained an amnesty for all the Quraish who abandoned armed resistance"(23). Save for a few irreconcilables (cf. Mubarrad, al-Kamil, ed. Wright, p. 365), they agreed, and thus the Prophet was able to enter into his native city practically without any resistance and almost all of its inhabitants accepted Islam. The Prophet performed the amnesty with great generosity and endeavored to win all hearts "by rich gifts (ta'lif al-qulub), a new use of the arms; cf. Q. ix. 60). (24). The Prophet only demanded destruction of all idols ruthlessly in and around Mecca. Commenting on this successful entry to the holy place Mecca, one author says, "Only Sura cx. seems to preserve an echo of the exaltation with which this victory filled him; here as in the unusually touching passage Q. xlviii. 1 sq. he sees in the success of this plan a sign that Allah has forgiven him all his sins"(25).

The Prophet did not rest long upon his emblem of victory for not only was Ta'if, which was closely related with Mecca, still not subdued, but the Hawazin tribes in Central Arabia were getting ready for a decisive fight. Thus, a war was fought with these Beduins at Hunain on the road to Ta'f which at the beginning appeared to be a disaster to the Prophet, primarily because of the unreliability of some new Muslims, until some of his followers successfully recalled those fugitives who routed the enemy completely (cf. Q. 9. 25 sq.). On the other hand, his inexperienced troops were unable to take Ta'if with its defenses. The people of Ta'if, however, later on fell in with the spirit or wave of the situation and adopted Islam. Following the victory at Ta'f, his followers thought that since the Prophet entered Mecca, he might stay in his native land leaving them behind unprotected and uncared for. But the Prophet spoke with extreme kindness to remove their conjecture; as a result, they burst into tears and declared their unconditional satisfaction.

The important features of the year 9/630-1 in the memory of the Muslims was the many embassies that came from different parts of Arabia to Madina, to submit on behalf of their tribes to the conqueror of Mecca (cf. Q. cx. 3) and the messengers who were sent by the Prophet to the tribes, laying down conditions of their adoption of Islam. In the following year, he planned to conduct a campaign against Northern Arabia on large scale, probably because of the setback in Transjordania to be avenged, and because the Ghassanid was adopting a hostile attitude toward the Prophet and his new religion (cf. Ibn Hisham, p. 911; Bukhari, maghazi b. 78f). But he did not have much support from his followers (cf. Q. 9. 45, 81-90, 98 sqq.). He also had considerable opposition in Madina (Q. 9. 58-72; 125). At that time, the Prophet took recourse to his usual way of warning for those who were not following his way, but he had the passion in Mecca (cf. Q. 9. 70, 128 sq.). Matters reached a situation when some of his old opponents like 'Amir 'Abd 'Amr, founded a separate house of prayer of their own "for division among the faithful and a support for those who had formerly fought against God and His Prophet"(Q. 9. 07 sqq.). In spite of all opposition, however, he carried through his plan, but when after great difficulty, he had reached Tabuk on the frontier, (in the land of the Byzantines), he stayed there for some time and then returned to Madina. "His prestige had now become so great that the petty Christian and Jewish states in the north of Arabia submitted to him during his stay in Tabuk, for example the Christian King Yuhanna in Aila, the people of Ajruh and the Jews in the port of Makna"(26).

These years showed a significant increase in the prestige of the ruler of Madina, the Prophet, abroad: Now Mecca also under his control, and among the Beduins there was an inclination in many places to submit to the will of the conqueror of this town, for sure, to be safe against his attacks and also to have a share in his rich booty. Even in regions so remote as Bahrein and Uman within the sphere of Persian influence, and among the chiefs of Arabia, the new teaching of the Prophet and discipline of things spread and found sincere followers in some places.

Despite the above-mentioned calm atmosphere, it will be wrong to assume that the whole population of those places adopted Islam. As regards open opponents, the question was quite simple: when they were heathens, adhered to their paganism and would not abandon their polytheism, so they were to be threatened by the Prophet with the "holy war". He had not only to deal with such as those in Arabia, but there were also in addition to the Jews, who had already felt his strength, a considerable number of Christians, and some Persis in the eastern and southern districts.

The Prophet was thus faced with a problem which he had to resolve. From the words of the Qur'an in sura 9. 29 sqq. where the Prophet includes the Jews and the Christians, the people of strict monotheism, among the polytheists, who give Allah a son and honour men as lords besides Him, one would expect that the Prophet would have fought them like the heathen if they did not adopt Islam (cf. Q. 9. 76 sqq). But in contrast to such utterances, we have another sura

5. 82 where he mentions the Christians politely because they, unlike the Jews, show themselves kindly towards true believers and are not angry, which the Prophet ascribes to the fact that they have priests and monks (Cf. in the Qur'an monasticism: sura 1vii. 27). Ultimately, the distinction between the Jews and Christians completely disappeared when their position was eventually settled. Happily, they were included together as "peoples of a scripture" and they were allowed to continue practicing their religion provided they recognise, in return, the political authority of the Prophet by paying the jizya, (tax on the ahl al-kitab), if they did not, they were to be fought without mercy. Commenting on the above-mentioned agreement, Buhl says, "The memory of the agreement between Muhammad 's teaching and that of the 'peoples of a scripture', earlier so much emphasized, must have contributed to this rather illogical settlement and in addition there was the fact that treating the Jews as tax-paying tenants, and allowing them to practice their religion, as had been already done at Khaibar, was much more practical for the Muslims than fighting them till they gave in" (27). There was a further compromise with the "peoples of a scripture" according to which they were allowed to marry the daughters of the "peoples of a scripture" and to eat food prepared by them (Q. 5. 5). It is important to note that the Parsis (Q. 22. 17) were included among the "peoples of scripture", which made a difficulty for better informed generations of the later ages. Probably for practical reasons, the Prophet did not ask them to give up their religion. This extended application of the term "peoples of the scriptures, is found not only in the Qur'an but also in a letter of the Prophet to the Parsis in Hajar, but with a limitation that the Muslims are forbidden to marry their women and eat meat killed by them.

The Prophet was soon looking forward to reaching the ultimate goal of his life: to form an ummat ul-muslimin purely on a religious basis because by that time the inhabitants of a number of areas of

Arabia were then actually bound together by religion—Islam. Hence the old differences among the Arab tribes with their endless tribal feuds, "their blood vengeance and their lampoons which continually stirred up new quarrels, were to disappear at the will of the Prophet Muhammad and all believers were to feel themselves brethren"(Q. 9. 11; xiix. 10). It is believed that the Prophet had in his mind this unity and brotherhood among his religious brothers, the Muslims, it took little bit of time to achieve his goal. Certainly there must not be any distinction among believer-brothers save in their degree of piety (Q. xiix. 13). Some say that the rapid expansion of Islam had been accompanied by a considerable "diminution" in its religious content. This is nothing but a thinking which happens only in the human process, but certainly not in the divine message, which is complete.

However, alongside of the older adherents, who were really carried away by the Prophet's preaching and whose faith had been tried by privations and dangers, there were now the many converts who had been gained primarily by fear or by the prospect of material advantages. Despite the teachers sent out to them, there could be no question of long-seated conversation among these Arabs, and now the old Arab spirit continued to flourish among them. The Prophet himself in sura xiix.14 has recorded very definitely how far the Beduins were from the faith: they cannot say that they believe but only that they have adopted Islam. Commenting on the lifestyle of the Prophet during those busy days, especially after his authority was established firmly in Mecca, Buhl says: "Commandments relating to religion and worship, which had considerably occupied Muhammad in the early Madinese period, give way in striking fashion to social and political regulations, a natural result of the fact that the new members were not rife for the formers" (28). Uncertainty on these matters was still great or endless. This is true even of so fundamental a law as the rules for the times of daily prayer, as the five-time prayers later were made obligatory, are nowhere laid down in the Qur'an. Some say that they were probably instituted by the Prophet himself towards the end of his life, but it is not very probable considering the fact that it was not mentioned in the Qur'an.

To be sure, only two religious institutions are mentioned in the Qur'an, for example, the hajj (pilgrimage to the sanctuaries at Mecca) and the 'umra in the town itself. For sure, the hajj was the crown of his endeavours begun in Mecca and carried through with utmost determination. The Prophet, now the ruler or master of Mecca, did not take part in the pilgrimage of the year 8, nor did he come to Mecca to perform the pilgrimage in the year 9, but he sent his representative, Abu Bakr, who read a proclamation with momentous results (cf. sura 9) but according to the usual tradition, it was 'Ali who acted as his (Prophet's) deputy, for which Abu Bakr is reported to have complained to the Prophet (cf. Tabari, i. 1760 sq.). There is another tradition, according to which Abu Bakr, commissioned Abu Huraira to proclaim the exclusion of the heathen from the hajj (cf. Abu Sa'd, 11/i. 121 sq.). This, what is known as the bara'a in which the Prophet, who had been for so many years excluded from the hajj, forbade all non-Muslims (heathens) any participation in it and granted them a period of four months, after the expiry of which they were given the choice between the adoption of Islam and severe warfare (Q. sura 9. 11 sqq). This explains the cause for his absence from the celebration during the two preceding years. He wanted to wait until he could celebrate it as the only ruler and totally in agreement with his intentions, as he himself said, with the ceremonies introduced by Abraham (Q. 2. 125 sq.).

Finally, all was ready and at the end of the year 10/March, 632, he was able to carry through the first reformed pilgrimage (the "Farewell Pilgrimage" or the "Pilgrimage of Islam") which became the "standards" or finally accepted for all time for all Muslims. Now, it is remarkable that the regulations for the regularisation of the hajj, the object of which was to remove all that was too openly pagan in the pre-Islamic ceremony (cf. e. g. the awthan in Mina, in Farazdaq, in ZDMG, 1ix. 604), and to give it Islamic features, but broadly speaking, the later form is most probably based on what the Prophet laid down on this remarkable occasion.

The Farewell Pilgrimage, at which an important and effective address is put in the Prophet's mouth, marks the highest point in his career. His feelings on that occasion are expressed in Allah's words in sura 5. 3: In addition to the rules forbidding food and drink, "This day have I perfected your religion for you and completed My favour unto you, and have chosen for you as religion AL-ISLAM". There is, therefore, a hint of the dramatic in the fact that his career ended only a months later. He himself hardly expected this because only a month before his death, he was preparing an expedition against Transjordania, under the command of Usama, in order to avenge the death of his father. It is also reported that the situation was so grave that it required a man in full force or energy to deal with it; in different places, the appearance of different "prophets" has provoked disturbances. Then suddenly the Prophet felt it, apparently from the ordinary Madina fever (cf. Farazdak, 9. 13), but this was dangerous for a man physically and mentally "overwrought". He recovered for a short time, but then died on the 13th Rabi' 1 of the year 9/June 8, 632, in the presence of his wife, 'A'isha'. "The wild confusion which party passions let loose in Madina when death became known had the remarkable result that his corpse remained neglected for a whole day until it was finally buried under 'A'sha's hut" (Tabari, i. 1817; Ibn Sa'ad, 11/ii. 57sqq., 71).

CHAPTER 2 : References

1. For Muhammad's whole life-history, cf. F. Buhl, "Mmuhammad", Shorter Encyclopaedia of Islam,(SEI), pp. 390-405.
2. Quoted in Schoeps, Hans-Joachim, The Religions of Mankind: Their Origin and Development, (Translated from the German by Richard and Clara Winston), Anchor Books, Doubleday & Company, Inc., Garden City, New York, 1968, P. 242.
3. Buhl, of. cit., pp. 392f.
4. Ibid.
5. Ibid.
6. Ibid.; also cf. sura, 10. 17, 21; 28. 85 sq.; 1xix. 44; 1xxv. 16 sq.; 7. 203; 16. 98; the convincing imparatives 1xxix. 2; xcvi. 1; the self-denunciation 1xxx. 1 sqq.
7. Ibid.
8. Ibid., p. 394.
9. Ibid., p. 395.
10. Ibid.
11. Ibid., p. 396.
12. Cf. B. Schrieke, "Isra', SEI.; J. Horovitz, "Mi'raj", SEI.
13. Buhl, op. cit., p. 396.
14. Ibid.
15. Ibid.
16. Ibid.
17. Ibid.
18. Ibid. For more information about the Prophet's attitude to the Jews, cf. Q. 9. 107.
19. Ibid.
20. Ibid., p. 400.

21. Ibid., P. 401.

22. Cf. Noldeke in WZKM, 21. 307; Goldziher, Vorlesungen uber den, Islam, p. 25, and T. W. Arnold, The Preaching of Islam, p. 23 sqq.

23. Cf. 'Urwa, Tabari, i. 1634 sq.

24. Buhl, op. cit. p. 402.

25. Ibid.

26. Ibid., p. 403.

27. op. cit.

28. op. cit., p. 404.

CHAPTER 3

Fundamental Principles of Islam

Shahada (testimony or belief): In the religious use of the word shahada is the Muslim profession or affirmation of faith in One Ultimate Reality (Allah): "There is no god but Allah". And by extension it is the testimony one gives in fighting for Islam, especially in dying for Islam in the holy war (jihad).

Therefore, the first of the Fundamental Principles or Pillars of Islam is belief (iman) in One Supreme God (Allah). He was one of the pre-Islamic Arabian supreme gods. However, the name is more likely of Aramaic origin—"alaha", the god.

From the Qur'anic verses, it becomes clear that Allah was a well-known god who was known as a creator and provider; they called him in times of danger; they used to swear by him, and they reserved for him a separate portion, unlike other deities (1).

However, in pre-Islamic Arabia, he was one of the many deities, but in Islam, He is the only One God. In Islam, Allah has ninetynine attributes. It is likely that the Prophet Muhammad was familiar with that god and his role in that society.

Therefore, Prophet Muhammad's God (Allah) was very significant for he did not fight with his countrymen at least for the name of his God, Allah. In fact, because of the name Allah, the only God of Islam, most Arabs found it easy to accept the Prophet's preaching for Islam with Allah as the ultimate Reality, even though this Allah's whole perspective is completely changed.

In a nutshell, in contradistinction to the pre-Islamic Arabian conception of Allah, the Prophet's Allah in Islam is the unparalleled supreme God. He is the Creator (<u>Al-khaliq</u>); The Destroyer (<u>Al-fani</u>); the Owner (<u>Al-Malik</u>) of the world; also He is The Merciful (<u>Al-Rahman</u>); The Compassionate (Al-Rahim). It should be emphasised that these are only four of the ninety-nine beautiful names (<u>al-asma' al-husna</u>) or epithets (<u>sifat</u>) of this Allah (2). The unity of Allah in Islamic belief is emphatically mentioned in these words in the Qur'an (sura 112) named <u>Al-tawhid</u>: "Say: He is Allah, the One! Allah, the eternally Besought of all! He begeteth not nor was He begotten. And there is none comparable unto Him"(3).

In Islam, Allah's absolute power and authority has been emphasised in many verses, along with Allah's diverse character. His might or power that controls everything from the universe to the individual, in all aspects is thus stated in the Qur'an: "Allah! There is no god save Him, The Alive, The Eternal. Neither slumber, nor sleep overtaketh Him. Unto Him belongeth whatsoever is in the heavens and whatsoever in the earth, who is he that intercedeth with Him save by His leave? He knoweth that which is in front of them and that which is behind them, while they encompass nothing of His knowledge save what He will. His throne includeth the heavens and the earth, and He is never weary of preserving them. He is the sublime, the Tremendous" (Q. 2. 255). Further, "Unto Allah [belongeth] whosoever is in the heaven, and whatsoever is in the earth, and whether ye make known what is in your minds or hide it, Allah will bring you to account for it. He will forgive whom He will, and He will punish whom He will. Allah is able to do all things" (Q. 2. 284). Many more similar attributes of Allah are found in other Qur'anic verses as well. Comparing and contrasting the pre-Islamic

Arabian (jahiliyah) social systems where there was no equality of men, even in the religious sphere, with that of the Islamic vis-à-vis Allah, Oshihiko Izutsu says: "Islam, on the contrary, stressed from the very outset the universal grace and goodness of Allah. The awful Lord of the Last Day is at the same time the most merciful and the most compassionate God, who makes no distinction at all between rich and poor, the powerful and the un-influential. In the presence of this God, all men are equal, irrespective of distinctions of rank and lineage". "Nay", concludes the learned author, "He even prefers the weak and insignificant to the arrogant aristocrats. 'O most merciful', as Muhammad prays, 'thou art indeed the Lord of the oppressed. Thou art my Lord'"(4).

On the basis of God's attributes, the Qur'an has unequivocally established an Ethical Monotheism for the "basic elan of the Qur'an is moral", says Fazlur Rahman, "whence flows its emphasis on monotheism as well as on social justice"(5). Dr. Rahman says further: "It is because of the Qur'an's paramount emphasis on the Moral Law and the Qur'anic God has seemed to many people to be primarily the God of Justice"(6). Notwithstanding the ethical aspect, as we have just mentioned above, if we consider the Qur'anic information, as a whole, we find more: "Indeed, the most intense impression that the Qur'an, as a whole, leaves upon a reader is not of a watchful frowning, and punishing God . . . nor of a chief judge . . . but of a unitary and purposive will creative of order in the universe: the qualities of power or majesty, of watchfulness or justice, and of wisdom attributed to God in the Qur'an with unmistakable emphasis are, in face, immediate inferences from the creative orderliness of the cosmos" (7). Considering the gradual development of the notion of Allah in the Qur'an, the writer says: "A concept of God, the absolute author of the universe, is developed where the attributes of creativity, order, and mercy are not merely conjoined . . . to one another but interpenetrated completely. To him [sic] belong creativity and 'ordering' or 'commanding' "(Q. 7. 54). Also Allah says "My mercy encompasses everything" (Q. 7. 156). "Indeed, the 'Merciful' (Rahman) is the only adjectival name of God that is very frequently used in the Qur'an as a substantive name of God besides Allah" (8). By the way, "Rahman was used as a name for the Deity in South Arabia before Islam, apart from Allah, as mentioned before.

Pre-Islamic Arabs also associated jinn with Allah. For example: "They asserted a 'kinship' (nasb) between Allah and the djinn"(9). Along with the pre-Islamic Allah, Islam has also integrated the concept of jinn, but not as a relative of Allah.

It is now adequately clear that having known the different aspects of the pre-Islamic pagan Arab concept of Allah and all his associates, such as angel, jinn and shaytan, the Prophet, with divine sanction (huqm), launched a mission, as Prophet and reformer, to preach a simple religion with Allah as the only Divinity without any partners and associates, for "the religion of Mecca in Muhammad's time was far from simple idolatry"(10). Having also known with both Judaism and Christianity, Prophet Muhammad considered himself as a "reformer" who was preaching Islam, as a religion basically or fundamentally in alliance with the two earlier Semitic divine religions, mentioned before. Therefore, his final knowing and understanding Allah is stated most simply in the first article of the crucial or essential Islamic creed: La ilaha illa Allah (There is no god save Allah). Commenting on this simple article of faith in Islam, D. B. Macdonald says: "This meant, for Muhammad and the Meccans, that of all the gods, whom they worshipped, Allah was the only real deity. It took no account of the nature of the God in the abstract, only of the personal position of Allah. "Allah, therefore, was and is the proper name of God among Muslims"(11). It is the same Allah who is Yahweh in the Biblical language.

At this stage it should be mentioned that there are other epithets of Allah describing His self-sufficiency and eternity. Prophet Muhammad praised Allah, the First (al-awwal); the Last(al-akhir); the Eternal (al-zahir); the Internal (al-batin) and the All-knowing (al-alim: Q. 57. 3); the Self-subsisting (al-Qayyum: Q. 2. 225; 3. 2). Allah is the One (al-wahud); The Living (al-haii: Q. 2. 225; 3. 2, etc); The Powerful (al-qadir : Q. 2. 20.); The Self-sufficing (al-ghani); The Absolute Originator (al-badi': Q. 2. 117; 6. 102); The Eternal (al-samad: Q. 112. 2); The Mighty (al-'aziz: Q. 59. 23f.; 3. 4; 6. 97); The Grand, Sublime, Tremendous ('ali al-'azim: Q. 2. 255); The Dominant (al-qahhar: Q. 12. 39); The Haughty (al-mutakabbir: Q. 59. 23); The Generous (al-karim): Q. 55. 78); The Strong (al-qawi); The Firm (al-matin: Q. 51. 58); The Aware (al-khabir: Q. 6. 104, 41); The Wise (al-hakim: Q. 3. 6, 97; 15. 25); The Hearer (al-sami': Q. 2. 256); The Seer (al-basir: Q. 17. 17, 30; 64. 2); The Holy King (al-malik-ul-quddus" Q. 59. 23; 62. 1). Allah is also the Best Judge (khayr al-hakimin: Q. 7. 87; 10. 109; 12. 8); He is also The Light of The Heaven and The Earth (al-nur: Q. 24. 35). Allah is The Forgiver (al-ghafur: Q. 5. 18); The Beneficient (al-rahim: Q. 59. 22); The Alive, The Eternal (al-hayy-ul-qayyum: Q. 2. 255; 3. 2); He is The Protector (al-hafiz: Q. 2. 286) (12).

The Prophet also used the word "Peace" (al salam: Q. 59. 23) for Allah and also His being "Light" as mentioned above. This, of course, is a Semitic description of God such as the "Light of the World" in the Gospel and "Light of Light' in the Nicene creed" (SEI). Allah is also described frequently in the Qur'an as "Real" or "Reality" (al-haqq); thus, the content of the message of the Qur'an to the Prophet Muhammad is described as "al-haqq min rabbika"(13): (Reality from your God).

In other words, the above-mentioned characteristics of God tell clearly that Allah is a Being Who is Self-sufficing, All-Knowing,

All-Encompassing, All-powerful, Eternal, and Who is the only Reality.

In passing, it may be mentioned that one of the attributes of Allah relating to His creation, is <u>Al-Bari'</u> the other is <u>Al-khaliq</u>, which evidently is taken by the Prophet/Islam from the Hebrew, "and is used without special meaning" (14). The above discussion concerning Allah's power in all matters comes down to this: Allah is the absolute Creator, Sustainer, Ruler-Destroyer, Restorer and Recorder; there is neither strength nor power except in Him alone.

In addition to the epithets described before, Allah has some characteristics mainly describing His relation to mankind. Therefore, Allah is The Compassionate or the Beneficent (<u>Al-rahman</u>) and The Merciful (<u>Al-rahim</u>). These are the two epithets Muslims use almost at every step of their lives. For sure, they are used at the beginning of each of the 113, out of 114, <u>suras</u> of the Qur'an, and the Muslims use them whenever and wherever they plan to do something, even eating and drinking, etc. Allah, for sure, is The Forgiver (<u>al-ghafir</u>: Q. 7. 155); The Much Forgiver (<u>al-ghafur, al-ghaffar</u>: Q. 20. 82); The Pardoner (<u>al-'afuuw</u>: Q. 4. 43); The Repenter (<u>al-tawwab</u>: Q. 2. 37); The Grateful, The Acknowledger of thanksgiving (<u>al-shakur</u>: Q. 35. 30); The Kind (<u>al-ra'uf</u>: Q. 2. 143); The Loving (<u>al-wadud</u>: Q. 11. 90); The Watcher (<u>al-raqib</u>: Q. 4, 1); The Reckoner (<u>al-hasib</u>: Q. 4. 86); The Witness (<u>al-shahid</u>; The Protector (<u>al-muhaimin</u>: Q.59. 23); The Guide (<u>al-hadi</u>; The Avenger or The Retributor (<u>al-muntaqim</u>: Q. 5. 95); The Giver (<u>al-wahhab</u>: Q. 3. 8); The Provider (al-razzaq: Q. 2. 57); and The Answerer of prayer (<u>al-mujib</u>: Q. 11. 61). Also cf. <u>sura</u> 30. 20-28.

Commenting on the above-mentioned qualities of Allah, Macdonald says: "Man's relation to Allah, there, is that of dependence. He needs Allah's forgiveness and patience. Allah is a Watcher and Rechoner over him; but he {sic} is also a faithful protector {sic} and guide {sic}. From him {sic} comes all sustenance in the widest sense. He does everything directly, hence these epithets, and, logically, no angels or intermediaries are needed in the scheme". Moreover, "And all by his {sic} will, 'he {sic} leadeth astray whom he {sic} wills, and guideth aright whom he {sic} wills' "(15).

It is sufficiently clear that Allah's varied attributes taught His messenger—the Prophet Muhammad—to be also flexible and dynamic, rather than inactive in his teachings and dealings with people, Muslim and non-Muslim. In fact, the whole Islamic system is distinguished by this character of liberalism, catholicism, flexibility, tolerance and understanding. Consequently, Muslims are bound, of necessity, to live by the precedent (sunna) of their instructor preceptor, the Prophet Muhammad, in every walk of their lives—religious, daily life, social, ethical, etc.—with necessary modifications as the circumstances require. By the way, this is called the dynamics of Islam.

Let us discuss here a few important matters about the Qur'an. Notwithstanding, we do not plan to discuss the whole history of the Qur'an per se, nor even all the matters discussed therein (cf, "al-Kor'an", SEI).

It should be mentioned here that Allah's flexibility is adequately found in the Qur'an; here there are instances of change not only in the earlier religions of divine revelation, but also in what had been earlier revealed to the Prophet Muhammad before being replaced by a later verse, under the concept of abrogating and abrogated (nasik and mansuk, respectively). The term goes back to Q. 2. 106, where it is said with reference to the change of the qibla (direction at prayer): "If We abrogate an aya or consign it to oblivion, We offer something better than it or something of equal value" (Q. 16. 101).

Considering all religious and historical sources, it is abundantly clear that the Qur'anic revelation is not totally new; rather, it is a continuation of the divine revelations that had been revealed to other Semitic messengers. It is stated in the Qur'an that the earlier scriptures of the Jews and Christians were based on the original heavenly or sacred books, so that they coincided partly with what is revealed to the Prophet Muhammad. The Qur'an "was sent down in perspicuous Arabic language and it is in the scriptures of the ancients; is it not a sign that the learned men of the Jews know it" (16).

Further, the Qur'an tells unmistakably the One Divine Scripture ('the mother of the scripture') which is held in the well-guarded tablet (35. 22) whence God revealed Himself in four consignments (17).

In accord with the above discussion concerning the Semitic background of the Qur'an, thus of Islam, no one should be surprised to find in the Qur'an names of so many Semitic messengers and their associates (18). There also are mentioned in the Qur'an names of some ancient clans and tribes (19).

Finally, there are some <u>suras</u> of the Qur'an named after some of those personalities and clans who either belonged to the Semitic tradition or related to it (20).

Following the above explanation of some of the elements and ideas of the Semitic tradition found in the Qur'an, it is finally established that the Qur'an, so is Islam, is not totally a new system; in fact, at least, partly, it is a continuation of the previous tradition. Commenting on the link between Islam and the previous monotheistic religion, Stewart says: "Throughout the later part of his [Muhammad] mission in Mecca, stories of Biblical figures were being added to the Qur'an. The most frequently mentioned is Mosses [Ar. <u>musa</u>] with

136 references. He is followed by Abraham [Ar. ibrahim] with 69, Noah [Ar. Nuh] with 43, and Jesus [Ar. 'isa] with 36" (21).

In addition, it may be mentioned emphatically that Islam being the last of the Semitic religions (world religion as well) deals not only with religious-spiritual matters of the believers (Semitic), but also with the total life concerns of mankind, of this world and the world hereafter. Consequently, in addition to what we have already dealt with above, the Qur'an contains information about some historical facts—ancient stories; legal, moral, social-communal matters; political and economic matters; family matters, particularly how to treat one's parents irrespective of their beliefs (cf. Q. 17. 23 ff.; 46. 15 ff.); man's relationship with all human beings even outside one's own family, that is to say, in the community or society at large; humanity such as respect for life, with some exceptions (such as killing man or animal for one's own safety); man's duty to Allah and to fellow human beings as well. Thus, reflecting on the basic emphasis of the Qur'an at the early stages, Fazlur Rahman says, "The verses in the early suras are charged with extraordinary deep and powerful 'psychological moments'; they have the character of brief but violent volcanic eruptions. A voice is crying from the very depths of life and impinging forcefully on the Prophet's mind in order to make itself explicit at the level of consciousness"(22). Although this feature of the Qur'an became a little milder later on, particularly at Medina where it deals with social-economic and political, legal and ethical issues of the newly formed Muslim Community (ummat-ul-muslimin) vis-a-vis other tribes and communities (Judeo-Christian, the pagan Arab tribes—the Aws and Khajraj, especially), still the content of the Qur'an remains forceful to deal with the existing situation—providing full direction on all matters. Thus a Madinese verse declares, "If We had sent down this Qur'an upon a mountain, you (O Muhammad) would have seen humbled, split asunder out of the fear of Allah. And those similitudes—We strike them for mankind; haply they reflect" (Q. 59. 21).

To throw more light on Allah's diverse actions <u>vis-a-vis</u> His creatures, particularly humans, His viceroy (Q. 2. 30 f., 34f.; 7. 10 ff.; 15-28-31; <u>et passim</u>), let us turn our attention to the statement of a Muslim modernist-writer who says, "We have explicitly stated . . . that the basic elan of the Qur'an is moral, from where flows its emphasis on monotheism as well as on social justice" (23). The moral law is Allah's 'Command'; man cannot make/do or undo it, and his duty is to submit to it as it is. To implement it man is required to perform service ('<u>ibada</u>) to Allah. However, in this matter, Allah has created a dilemma for man, as will be discussed later.

The moral law and social justice of Allah that man must perform in every step of his/her life, is regularly disturbed by the devil (<u>iblis/shaytan</u>). (cf. "Iblis, Satan", <u>SEI</u>), who as an angel (<u>jinn</u>) was opposed to the creation of Adam, to begin with, and who played a trick in getting Adam and Eve out of paradise (cf. 2. 36ff.; 15. 29-33, <u>et passim</u>, with Allah's implied permission), then got clear permission (<u>huqm</u>) from Allah to mislead mankind at every step of his/her life (cf. Q. 7. 14-18; 38. 76-85). Thus, man's readiness to follow God's Commandments, on the one hand, and <u>shaytan's</u> continuous tempting to stop him from doing anything good in the name of Allah and His agents, Man, and his society, on the other hand, have created moral dualism in man's character, which allows rise to moral fight. In a nutshell, on the one hand, Allah asked man to stay away from satanic influences, and, on the other, He allowed <u>satan</u> not to leave man free of his illusion or deception. This is an example of the universality of Allah's dynamic nature. Moreover, in addition to the story of <u>iblis vis-a-vis</u> man, The Qur'an tells of man's character in the following words: "Lo! We offered the trust to the heaven and the earth and the mountains, but they shrank from hearing it [the Qur'an/revelation] and were afraid of it. And man assumed it. Lo! He hath proved a tyrant and a fool" (33. 72). Speaking about the multifarious character of man, Fazlur Rahman says, "There can be hardly a more penetrating and effective characterization of the human situation and man's frail and faltering nature, yet his innate boldness and the will to transcend the actual towards the ideal constitutes his uniqueness and greatness"(24). In the light of that situation, to protect man, Allah's vicegerent, from Shaytan's tricks or beguilement, and Muhammad being the last of them, was given Allah's scripture—the Qur'an (cf. Q. 56. 77 f.; 85. 21 f.).

Before closing this subject, let us bring forward a statement about the revelations Prophet Muhammad received in contrast to the situation in the case of Jesus. The author emphatically brings to our attention the distinctive mark of Islam in these words: "The revelation is not actually a living experience between God and man, a happening into which God himself [sic] enters; but it is a book. The first word of Muhammad's revelation is "Read"! The page of the book is shown to him, the book the angel has brought down from heaven"(25). That is to say, in contrast to Jesus, who left no written word to his followers, Islam is a book-religion from the first moment on. God did not come down from heaven and give Himself to man; rather, He revealed a book—the Qur'an.

(B) salat (Five Daily Ritual Prayers)—the Second Pillar of Islam. The significance of this ritual prayer can be grasped plainly since it comes almost always after the First Pillar: tawhid (shahada). Although this is not found in the pre-Islamic literature; it is believed that the Prophet Muhammad took it from the Judaic-Christian tradition of Arabia. However, Wensinck has suggested an Aramaic influence in these words: "It is used in several Aramaic dialects for ritual prayer, which in Syriac at least is usually called ba'uta. Muhammad took over the word <u>salat</u> in this sense from his neighbours, and the Muslim's <u>salat</u> shows in its composition a similarity with Jewish and Christian service . . ." (26).

The obligatory prayers have some rituals to be performed before actually praying: At first, they are preceded by ritual ablution (<u>tahara/wadu'</u> or even <u>gusul</u> under certain circumstance (27). As a matter of fact, to perform this prayer, one must have not only a <u>pak</u> (purified) body but also clothing and even the place of prayer, such as a mosque or a family home, must be pure. To make sure about the purity of the place, one may even put on a pure piece of cloth or the best is to spread a <u>musulla</u> (jainamaj. In fact, in the language of jurisprudence (<u>fiqh</u>), it is stated as, "when the condition is amiss, the conditioned is amiss"(<u>idha fata al-shart, fata al-mashrut</u>). According to jurists, since this requirement of <u>tahara</u> belongs to the Madinese period, Jewish influence on it is possible. However, despite the hard condition, mentioned above, Allah has allowed flexibility under certain circumstances. Thus the Qur'an says: "O who believe! And if you are sick or on a journey, or one of you cometh from the closet, or ye have had contact with women (sexually), and ye find no water, then go to clean high ground and rub your faces and your hands with some of it to do (<u>tayammum</u>). Allah would not place a burden on you, but He would purify you and would perfect His grace upon you, that ye may give thanks (4. 43); also cf. 5. 6) (28). Here is a wonderful example of Allah's <u>rahmat</u> (grace) for allowing an alternative even for what is obligatory.

Although there is no specific direction found in the Qur'an for performing the obligatory prayers, nonetheless, it is established by the Prophet himself as found in the <u>hadith</u> (29). However, there are concessions even for obligatory prayers under certain circumstances. For example, a sick person is allowed to shorten his/her prayer as a travaller, or perform his/her prayers sitting or even lying as the physical conditions require. Similarly, a person is allowed to shorten (qasar) or even escape his/her prayer while travelling or on a battlefield. Then a person is permitted to perform his/her obligatory prayers as qada (belated),(30). Women are allowed to miss completely their obligatory prayers during their monthly menstruating period (haid) and post-child birth period of forty days (nifas) (31). There is another liberal concession even for the obligatory prayers. A person is permitted to defer his/her obligatory prayers to a later time if there is a life-threatening situation: for instance, at the battlefield soldiers are allowed to either delay the timely prayers or even postpone completely until either the war is over or the army has gone to a safer land (cf. Q. 2. 239; 9. 122). Finally, is the case of a terminally ill person—mental or physical—a person is allowed to drop obligatory prayers totally; however, he/she is under obligation to pay kaffara (restitution) but only if capable of doing so.

As the shahada, the right of salat (obligatory prayer) was an integral part of Islamic tradition, since the beginning (32). It may be mentioned here that the performance of the daily obligatory prayers as such, in Islam is a continuation from the ahl al-kitab who performed their daily prayers. Here we may draw your attention to an interesting historical fact: it is reported in the Tradition that on the occasion of his "Nocturnal Journey"(isra wa mi'raj) (33), Prophet Muhammad was allotted by Allah fifty (50) times of prayers a day. However, on his return, Prophet Muhammad met Prophet Moses at Jerusalem, who suggested that the Prophet Muhammad should go back to the Almighty Allah and request for only five (5) times of prayer a day rather than fifty. According to the Tradition (hadith), it was done as Moses suggested. Further, referring to the Qur'anic verse 2. 238, Wensinck holds: ". . . the middle salat (al-wasta) . . . must therefore have been added in Madina to the two usual salats and probably after the example of the Jews, who also performed tefilla three times a day" (34).

In this connection, attention should be drawn to an unprecedented surprising order of Allah Who has ordered the Muslims to show by action a conciliatory or friendly attitude by following a middle path even in performing their obligatory rights like the salat, so that the pagan Arabs, the life-long opponents of Islam, are not disturbed. "Say (unto mankind): Cry unto Allah, or cry unto the beneficent, unto whichever ye cry (it is the same). His are the most beautiful names. And thou (Muhammad), be not loud voiced in thy worship nor yet silent therein, but follow a way between"(Q. 17. 110). Commenting on the above-mentioned revelation, Wensinck says, "This is in agreement with the fact that in the period during which Muhammad is continually advised to imitate the examples of the earlier prophets and model himself on their patience, attention is regularly called to their also having summoned those around them to hold the salat"(35). By the way, following the above-mentioned Qur'anic injunction, there is an authentic (sahi) hadith which says: khayr al-amr awsatkum(your best way is the middle way). *In fact, this hadith is in confirmation of the Qur'nic verse: "when you spend, neither show off nor cut off, for you there is a middle way" (Q.25. 67)*.The last word about the prayer, is that the salat is also called an expression of humility (cf. Q. 23. 2), which was considered in Hellenistic (Greek) tradition as the attitude to the deity most befitting man. This, of course, is true in all traditions, notwithstanding the difference in the ways of expression.

About the five daily ritual prayers, it is quite interesting to take note that the revelations in this connection have been varied and different to the extent of allowing maximum flexibility throughout the course of development to reach the last number. Since there is not one verse establishing the five daily fard (obligatory) prayers, it is abundantly clear that Allah intended to make the Islamic system to be progressive and gradual so that the follower of it (the Muslim) can easily get used to it.

In this connection, it may be mentioned that neither during the Meccan period of the Prophet (610-622) nor during the Madinine period (622-632) no one verse established all five daily obligatory prayers. Notwithstanding, the following are the relevant verses establishing the daily ritual prayers: for example, sura 11. 114 says: "Establish salat at the two ends of the day as well as some watches of the night". Sura 17. 78 confirms fundamentally with this even though it has a different wording: "Establish salat at the going down of the sun until the dark of the night, and the recital of the Qur'an [salat] at dawn". And in sura 24. 58 "salat of fajar" (dawn prayer) and the "salat al-'isha" (night prayer) are mentioned. Then we find in the Madinine sura 2. 238 the mention of the salat al-wusta (the middlde prayer). This addition is most probably following the example of the mid-day Jewish prayer, as mentioned before. According to the mufassirin (exegetical opinion), the plural word salawat in the above verse means all salats in general, rather than only the five obligatory (fard) ones.

The above-mentioned explanation about the salat shows that the Islamic system is open to adopting good examples or elements from the pre-Islamic traditions, particularly Jewish or Hebrew. But I. Goldzihar suggests a Persian influence in setting the daily ritual prayers at five times (36).

As for the actual performance of the daily obligatory prayers, Prophet Muhammad himself was said to have shown flexibility even under regular conditions. Thus, Ibn 'Abbas reports that The Prophet combined together in Madina several prayers; for instance, the midday (zuhar) and late afternoon ('asr) at one time and the evening (maghrib) and night ('isha') at another time even though he was at home under normal circumstances. At any rate, there are ahadith (traditions) bringing the conclusion that the number of daily prayers had not been fixed at five during the Prophet's lifetime (37).

It may be pointed out here that the name <u>salat al-maghrib</u> is probably a borrowed name from the Jewish <u>ma'arib</u> (evening prayer), with this difference: while the former is performed only at dusk (not actually sunset), the latter is performed in the late afternoon or early evening without any reference to the sunset.

Finally, it should be mentioned that the Friday congregational prayer is made obligatory by the Qur'anic verse 62. 9 in these words: "O ye who believe! When the call is heard for the prayer of the day of congregation {<u>jum'a</u>}, haste unto remembrance of Allah and leave your trading. That is better for you if ye did but know (38).

Notwithstanding the obligatory performance of this prayer, there are a few conditions such as these: one must be a free Muslim, healthy, adult, male, resident (not travelling), of a city and a Muslim country.

For the weekly congregation, the religious significance of Friday has some similarity to the Jewish Sabbath and the Christian Sunday. However, unlike the Jewish Sabbath or the Christian Sunday, in Islam Friday is not a rest day, for the Qur'an says: "And when the prayer is ended, then disperse in the land and seek of Allah's bounty, and remember Allah much, that ye may be successful"(62. 10). Nevertheless, it appears that Islam could not progress without absorbing some elements from the other tradition already in operation. For example, beginning from the late "Umayyad period, the ceremonies of the Friday service became more and more influenced by the Christian service. Thus the ceremony of <u>adhan</u> (which is held once more in the mosque, after the faithful are gathered there before the sermon) and the peculiar form of <u>khutbah</u>, in two sections before the Friday <u>salat</u>, seem to have arisen under the influence of the Christian mass"(39). Eventually, the <u>mullah</u> (preacher) replaced the khutbah and in some places his governor, as the imam (conductor) of the prayer and started acting like a priest ever since.

(C) sawm (Fasting): The meaning of the word sawm in Arabic is "to be at rest", as we will see later. The history and practice of fasting in Islam began after the hijra to Madina in 622 C. E. According to C. Creg, "The meaning of the word 'fasting' may have been taken from Judaic-Aramaic usage, when Muhammad became better acquainted with the institution of fasting in Madina" (cf. "Sawm", SEI).

The word sawm occurs once in the Qur'an, referring to Maryam (mary), in the Meccan sura 19. 26, where it says, "So eat and drink and be consoled. And if you meetest . . . Say: Lo! I have vowed to fast unto the Beneficent, and may not speak . . ."

The word sawm is interpreted by the commentators as samt ("silence"). It is suggested that the Prophet Muhammad may have observed the "Christian practice keeping silence while fasting". Nevertheless, it is only after the hijrat that he asked his followers to fast on the 'Ashura' day, obviously, following the Jewish practice in Madina"(40). That is to say, he copied the Jewish fast of tishri. However, this was only a voluntary fasting day observed on the 10th Muharram. 'Ashura' of Hebraic-Aramaic origin, as in Lev.16. 29, is used on the Day of Atonement. Prophet Muhammad having been acquainted with this fast, "retained the Jewish practice in the rite, that is, the fast was observed on this day from sunset to sunset . . ." (41). However, in the second year of the hijrat (624) following the breakdown of the Muslim-Jewish relations, the Prophet looked for the alternative fasting time. At that crucial time, "the Muslim fast, "under the influence of the Christian Quadragesima was turned into an abstinence of one lunar month's duration, that of Ramadan, which in the ancient Arab calendar with its solar correction, fell in Summer . . ." (42). Anyway, at the same time came the revelation of <u>surah</u> 2.183-85 abolishing the '<u>Ashura</u>' fast as an obligation and institutionalising, in its place, the fast of the Arabic lunar month of Ramadan. However, some orthodox Muslims, particularly ladies, are still practicing the 'Ashura' fasting.

As for the obligatory fast in the month of Ramadan in which the Qur'an was sent down from the "Guarded Tablet" to the world sky (cf. Q. 2. 185; 85. 21f.; 97. 1) to be revealed to the Prophet Muhammad during his 23-year prophetic life. Thus, in honour of the month of Ramadan, every mature Muslim man and woman must fast for the whole month of Ramadan from dawn to dusk (cf. Q. 2. 183ff.). According to F. Goitein, "the above-mentioned verse of the Qur'an (especially2. 183) calls attention to the parallelism between the mission of Muhammad and handing of the tablets of the law of Moses, which according to Jewish tradition took place on the Day of Atonement ('<u>Ashura</u>', the predecessor of of Ramadan) and actually was the cause of its institution" (43). The first step or alternative to replace the '<u>Ashura</u>' was a period of ten days of penance of the Jews preceding the Day of Atonement and continues to the present day in the ten days of the <u>i'tikaf</u>'. However, the Qur'anic verses of 2. 183 and 2. 187 finally corrected the Muslim Ramadan Fasting period from dawn to nightfall (dusk) (44).

It should be stated emphatically that the ritual of fasting imposes complete abstention (<u>imsak</u>) from all acts of normal life such as food, drink, sexual life and drugs. In fact, the whole code of ethics and morality is applied. All enjoyable works like gambling and smoking, drinking alcohol and all reprehensible works are forbidden. However, Islamic liberalism tolerates any forbidden act if it is done unintentionally; only ransom and repentance are required (45).

Notwithstanding that the <u>sawm</u> of Ramadan is an obligatory (<u>fard</u>) ritual, Allah has granted special exemption for some people under certain circumstances (cf. Q.2. 184f.), especially 185, which says: ". . . . Allah desireth for you ease; He desireth not hardship for you; . . ." Taking lead from the Qur'anic verses, the fuqaha (jurists) completed the list of exemptions, showing the flexibility of Islam even in the obligatory rite like sawm. It should be mentioned that the people who are exempted from it fully are those who are not in a normal mental health condition (gayr 'aqil). Also temporary exemptions have been granted to those who are in ill health (marid), or traveling (musafir); at war, or out of provisions, or in the case of women, in a state of menstruation (haid), or during the forty days after childbirth (nifas). However, these temporary exemptions must be compensated for later for an equivalent period (cf. Q. 2. 184 f.). However, those who are terminally ill, but in normal mental health ('aqil), have to pay a ransom—the feeding of a [Muslim] person, if only they can afford it for each fast (cf. Q. 2. 184).

In passing, an important feature of Islamic civilization should be mentioned here: Considering human vulnerability to forgetfulness, in taking their food on time or even living a comfortable family life, such as having intercourse with one's wife during the night of the fasting days, Allah has granted extremely benevolent concession by revealing the verse 2. 187: "It is made lawful for you to go unto your wives on the night of the fast. They are raiment for you and ye are raiment for them. Allah is aware that ye were deceiving yourselves in this respect and He hath turned in mercy towards you. So hold intercourse with them and seek that which Allah hath ordained for you, and eat and drink until the white thread becometh distinct from the black thread of the dawn. Then strictly observe the fast till nightfall and touch them not, but be at your devotions in the mosque. These are the limits imposed by Allah, so approach them not . . .".

In addition to the spiritual values, fasting has also physical significance. To be sure, fasting can help one to maintain a good physical condition especially the fatten condition; fasting also helps people to develop the habit of endurance particularly under the food shortage situation. In practical condition, fasting develops the quality of humanism in consideration of the millions of the world's people who suffer almost always from food shortages, especially on the continent of Africa. Thus, talking in terms of physical and psychological experience, "fasting is an inestimable lesson for the fasting Muslims to be more humane and kindhearted towards their fellow-human beings". "Some medical professionals advise their patients", continues the learned author, "who have either the tendency to obesity or are already suffering from it, to control their diet. Just doing this, which obviously does not involve complete fasting, yet arrests obesity. For diarrhea or chronic stomach ailments, doctors usually prescribe diet control, though not total fasting or abstinence from provisions"(46).

In addition to what is stated above, the fasting in Islam during the daytime, the time for eating, drinking and having fun or merrymaking, not sleeping, as at night, teaches us how to be the controller of our body and mind rather than their order-carrier or servant.

(D)—Jakat (Compulsory Poor Tax): The forth obligatory payment is zakat (poor tax), levied only on rich Muslims (ahl-i-nisab) which is distributed among poor Muslims, to begin with, then among other Muslims only in accord with particular rules and circumstances as prescribed in the Qur'an (cf. 2. 43; 9. 58, 60 and 79). There must not be any misconception between the zakat and the modern time income tax, which is paid on income rather than on total savings—the superfluous.

According to Joseph Schacht, Zakat (the institution) became known to the Prophet Muhammad from the Jewish tradition. "In Aramaic, the word zakat is used by the religious people to mean giving away of worldly possessions . . . as a particularly pious act. The possession of earthly riches is regarded almost as an obstacle to salvation; the same word that denoted virtue and righteousness in general could therefore also be used for benevolence and charitable gifts"(47). In his dynamic lifestyle, Prophet Muhammad must have become familiar with this kind of piety. Therefore, from the beginning, the Qur'an emphasised the practice of benevolence as one of the primary virtues of the real Muslim (cf. Q. 13. 22; 35, 29; 74. 24 f.; 76. 8f.).

Throughout the Meccan period, emphasis is placed unabated on two points: "Giving away, secretly and openly, from one's wealth, to particular individuals, viz., the beggar and the destitutes" (70. 25; also cf. 2. 177, 215). "And feed with food the needy wretch, the orphan and the prisoner, for love of Him, (saying): we feed you for the sake of Allah only. We wish for no reward nor thanks from you" (Q. 76. 8f.). Since it is an obligatory poor-tax, it is meant only for the right classes of people, mentioned in the Qur'an (2. 177, 215; 9. 60).

According to Schacht, ". . . already to the Meccan period belongs the use of the zakat along with several derivatives of the root zaka 'to be pure' which to the Arab mind were related to it". Speaking more on this subject, Schacht says, "Even the latter have in the Kor'an almost exclusively the meaning 'to be pious', which is not pure Arabic, but going back to the Jewish religion" (48). The encouragement of a compulsory poor tax comes also from the background of what the Muslims saw in their neighbourhood, the price of holding or hoarding under those circumstances, the Muslims frequently asked the Prophet as to "what they ought to spend. Say: That which is superfluous" (Q. 2. 219). As a matter of fact, a later revelation threatens those who hoarded with the punishment of hell (9. 34 ff.).

In any case, throughout the Qur'an the word <u>zakat</u> is used more than one simple meaning, such as "give poor tax"; rather, it is used in other related meanings, even though in general it means "virtue" (Q. 7. 156; 19. 31; 21. 73; 23. 4; 30. 39; 31. 4; 41. 7; 87. 14).

It is clear from the above-mentioned verses that in the Qur'an, the word <u>zakat</u> is not used always to denote only one thing. Nevertheless, the fundamental idea is giving away something from one's surplus or superfluous possessions, in order to purify oneself or to achieve <u>nek</u> (virtue). By the way, the same idea was in vogue among the Jews and among the pre-Islamic Arabs. Hence, commenting on the payment of the zakat by the Jews and the Arabs as a way of avoiding the evil spirit, Gaudefroy-Demombynes says: "For the Arabs, as for the Jews, worldly possessions may be a gift of the spirit of evil and foreshadow the lasting sufferings of the other life. But there is a way of avoiding this danger"(49). Considering further the issue of the use of the words <u>zakat</u> and <u>sadaqa</u>, (Hebrew <u>tzedaka</u>) as a purifying act, by both Jews and Muslims, the above-mentioned writer says: "If a man voluntarily gives back to Allah a part of the possessions that He has Himself given, by the act he 'purifies what he retains' . . ."(50).

Further, it should be stated here clearly that Allah has not imposed <u>zakat</u> as a compulsory poor tax on all Muslims, nor has He made it obligatory on all items, rather only a few, and only on those rich Muslims who have made a net saving of ten (10) <u>dirhams</u> (Arabian currency) at the end of the year (lunar year) and who would pay only two and half percent to the poor (<u>gharib/faqir</u>) Muslims. This was the rule since the time of the Prophet. It should be mentioned here that a particular portion of the <u>zakat</u> was reserved for the people of Mecca, the former adversaries of Islam, who converted <u>en masse</u> after the conquest of that city in 630 C. E., and whose hearts were to be reconciled (cf. Q. 9. 60). By doing that, it should be emphasised, the Prophet Muhammad exemplified his good will and gesture, thus made a conciliatory act towards his former home-born enemies in the name of Islam. Notwithstanding, eventually the shari'a has chalked out an elaborate rules administering the matters of zakat. Following that, at the beginning, the government collected the zakat without actually finding out one's actual income and saving; on the contrary, the zakat collectors depended fully on the truthfulness of the zakat payers. That was, in fact, a show of Islamic liberalism and open-mindedness. The government, it should be stated emphatically, responsibly distributed the collected zakat-money among the persons in accord with the Qur'anic injunction, as discussed above.

It should be stated here that as the Muslim territory expanded to become an empire, the government abandoned its responsibility as zakat-collector and, of course, distributor, leaving it completely to the care of the individual zakat-payer to pay as well as distribute among those mentioned in the Qur'an. Undoubtedly, this is an eye-opening example of Islamic liberalism and individualistic responsibility. Furthermore, in a non-priestly community, as the Muslim umma is, developing self-awareness concerning obligatory actions, is undoubtedly a God-given gift for the Muslims—to pay the zakat, as they individually realize the obligation (51). It should be mentioned here that as a matter of fact, there has never been any official interference in the matter of zakat-payment and distributions.

It may be mentioned here that the word sadaqa (to speak the truth) meaning that alms-giving by a Muslim is a kind of witness to the truthfulness of his/her religious faith. Notwithstanding, the Hebrew word tzedaka (whence the Arabic word sadaqa is drawn), means "honesty", and was later on used to mean "alms-giving". All these words together mean "Alms-giving honestly". In other words, although sadaqa is a voluntary alms-giving, it must be an honest act of charity, rather than a means of self-aggrandisement.

Finally, the significance of this voluntary alms can be achieved from the number of the Qur'anic verses where it is mentioned, alone or as a synonym of <u>zakat</u> (52). Paying <u>sadaqa</u> was practised by the pre-Islamic Arabs as well as by other Semitic peoples. It is a matter of ethics rather than obligation, as stated before. Therefore, Islam being an ethical monotheism, borrowing and adopting ethical lessons from other cultures, particularly from its own Semitic-Arab culture, is normal.

It is well-known that the Prophet Muhammad was a "paradigmatic" person of his Arab culture or heritage. Thus, we are told that the personal features attributed to him in the <u>Hadith</u> literature are in accord with the old nomadic ideals of man. For instance, Ibn Hisham writes in his <u>sirah</u>, on the authority of 'Ali ibn Abi Talib: "He was of all men the most open-handed, most stout-hearted, most truthful of tongue, . . ." (53).

One of the outstanding ethical characters of the pre-Islamic Arabia (<u>jahiliyyah waqt</u>) is popularly known have been <u>muruwwa</u>, and one of the many virtues included under that word was generosity (54). In the desert land, where even the essential things of life are not easily available, hospitality is extremely essential feature of life. Therefore, hospitality was one of the important characters of tribal solidarity. Thus, generosity was known to be "a master passion of the Arabs" (55). In passing, in this connection we may recall the name of the legendary Hatim Tai, recognsed as a super example of the Bedouin ideals of generosity and hospitality. It is also well-known that in ancient Arabia, well-known generous people were sometimes addressed as <u>Karim</u> (one of the epithets of Allah for His generosity in every respect to His '<u>abids</u>, worshippers).

Thus, following his Arab tradition, Prophet Muhammad showed "generosity using the economic principle for his religious-political

Community (<u>ummah</u>)". Nevertheless, the main difference between the two positions is this: Islam does not accept any act of generosity in order to make a show of one's wealth, "to demonstrate one's wealth and position in the society as a form of boasting, 'Dandyism' or chivalry for its own sake was in this view nothing but a satanic passion . . . All acts of generosity are absolutely valueless that came from the source of vainglory and pride" (56). In the same tune, we find in the Qur'an: "O ye who believe! Render not vain your alms-giving by reproach and injury, like him who spendeth his wealth only to be seen by men and believeth not in Allah and the Last Day. His likeness is as the likeness of a rock whereon is the dust of earth; a rainstorm smitten it, leaving it smooth and bare. They have no control of aught of that which they have gained. Allah guideth not the disbelieving folk" (Q. 2. 264). In other verses a lavish spender or a prodigal (<u>musrif</u>) is, in fact, declared <u>shaytan</u>'s brother: "Give the kinsmen his due, and the needy, and the wayfarer, and squander not (thy wealth) in wantonness". "Lo! The squanderers were ever brothers of the devil, and the devil was ever an ingrate to his Lord" (Q. 2. 26f.).

Praising the middle way that Islam imposes, even in the case of moral excellence like paying the <u>sadaqa</u>, Izutsu says: "Niggardliness is a moral defect or vice. But the excess of lavishness is no less a dishonourable moral defect, keep always to the happy medium; this is the rule of conduct that must control believers in matters concerning private property" (57). In line with these Qur'anic verses, there is a <u>hadith</u> which says, "your best way is the middle way" (<u>khayr al-omur awsatkom</u>).

Before closing this subject, let us put emphasis on the significance of the <u>sadaqa</u> by quoting some verses of the Qur'an (cf. 9. 58 ff., 103f.; 2. 195, 215, 219, 261-65, 277-74; 3. 92; 4. 114; 25. 67; 58. 12; 63. 100; 64. 16; 65. 7.). To begin with, the believers are encouraged to spend (nafaq) in the way of Allah out of pure kindness; the Qur'an warns the defaulter in these words: "Ye will not attain unto piety until you spend, Allah is aware thereof" (3. 92). Second, Allah warns the squanderers in the strongest language, calling them . . . "brothers of Satan . . ." (17. 22; also cf. 4. 29 f.; 38; 7. 7, 26). Third, Allah has also warned against miserliness (bakhil) in this way: The believers are told that bakhil (miser) will not be qualified to enter the paradise. We, therefore, come to the conclusion that even in the case of a nek (virtue) such as paying sadaqa, we cannot go to either of the two extremes—viz. to pay excessively (israf: Q. 7. 31), on the other hand, not to pay at all (bukhl).

To conclude: The fundamental principle of Islam is to do one's obligations in moderation—including sadaqa. This is what Allah has imposed on the Muslims in these words: "Keep not thy hand faltered to thy neck, nor yet spread it out too widely, lest thou shouldst become an object of reproach or stripped naked. Lo! Thy Lord spread out His provision to whomsoever He will or again straitens it as He will" (Q. 17. 29f.). From these verses, we can draw conclusion that the Islamic ideal is the middle way, as stated before.

E: Al-Hajj: (The Pilgrimage): This is the fifth of the Fundamental Principles of Islam. As in the case of Zakat, so is the case of the Hajj. This is another important example of Islam's liberalism even in the case of an obligatory duty. Therefore, Islam has made the hajj only once in the lifetime of a rich Muslim man and woman (maldar/ahl al-nisab). In this case, an extremely interesting act of Islamic liberalism must be recognised. At the beginning, Islam allowed the non-Muslims to perform the hajj, as they had done before. However, it was on condition that they had to make a particular treaty with the Prophet Muhammad. Thus, the Qur'an says, "Freedom from obligation (is proclaimed) from Allah and His messenger towards those of the idolaters with whom you made a treaty. Travel freely in the land for four months, and know that ye cannot escape Allah, and that Allah will confound the believers (in His guidance) . . . So, if ye repent, it will be better for you . . ." (Q. 9. 1-3).

Comparing the obligation of the zakat and the hajj, it is easy to understand why the former is an annual obligation and the latter is only once in one's lifetime: the former is one of the ways to help the less fortunate Muslim brothers in one's community, while the latter requires one to undertake a long journey to Saudi Arabia which often is very difficult, especially for the elderly hajis (pilgrims) when the hajj takes place in summer (cf. Q. 3. 97). Hence, reflecting on the origins and significance of the hajj in Islam, G-Demombynes says, "The pilgrimage is an institution of peculiar interest to the Muslim religion: Firstly, because it is a revival and a syncretism of ancient rites common throughout the Semitic East (Q. 2. 125-27), and also because gathering together in a great annual assembly, a throng of tens of thousands of the faithful from all parts of the world, it is the only real bond that unites the different Muslim communities, and the opportunity for a pan-Islamic reunion" (58).

Looking back at the history of pilgrimage before Islam, we see both pagan Arab and Hebrew roots. By the way, in Arabic the word hajj means "to betake oneself to"; and in Hebrew, it means to go around, to go in a circle". (59).This is actually what is done in the Muslim hajj, with a little difference. In pre-Islamic Arabia, annual fairs used to be held in the month of Dhu al-Qa'ida at 'Ukaz and Majanna in the present-day Sa'udi 'Arabia. However, despite the link with both the pagan Arab and Semitic tradition, (cf. Exd. 23. 14, 17; 34. 23), the Muslim hajj is a continuation of those rituals and customs, mutatis mutandis. In addition to the bazars or fairs, mentioned above, in pre-Islamic Arabia pilgrimage—type of festivals used to be held, not only in Arafat, but also in sanctuaries in northern Arabia—Petra and Palmyra, in the present day Kingdom of Jordan.

But, for Islam, "the first sanctuary appointed for mankind was that of Becca (Mecca), a blessed place, a guidance to the people" (Q. 2. 125 ff.; 3. 96; also cf. 97).

By the way, the idea of both holy months and holy places is pre-Islamic. For example, the three consecutive months of Dhu al-Qa'da, Dhu al-Hajj and Moharram formed a sacred period during which all tribal hostilities were put to rest, and no killing of any life within the holy territories. That peaceful atmosphere was helpful for holding the rite of pilgrimage which ended at the field of Arafat on the 9th of Dhu al-Hajj. Interestingly, Islam has adopted not only the Jahiliyya Arab lunar-calendar consisting of 12 months (cf. Q. 9. 36f.; also cf. 2. 189; 9. 2), but has also adopted the Arab sacred months, mentioned before, adding to them just one more month, the Ramadan, for a total of four sacred months (cf. Q. 9. 2, 36). Furthermore, there is another interesting element which Islam has adopted from the pre-Islamic Arab custom of "no feuds during the sacred months" (cf. Q. 2. 197, 217; 5. 1 f.; 9. 36 f.) and finally fixed the date for the annual pilgrimage on the 9th of Dhu al-Hajj, as the pre-Islamic Arabs did. Islam has adopted another pre-Islamic pilgrimage ritual—the halt (wuquf) in the field of Arafat. Interestingly, this halt has similarity to the stay of the Israilites on Mount Sainai (cf. Exd. 19. 15). Interestingly enough, like the Isreilites, the Muslims also follow other prohibitions in this regard. (60).

Further, in the pre-Islamic pilgrimage, there was the custom of maintaining the state of ihram (sanctification); Islam also has adopted this practice, which continues from the first day of the hajj (7th of Dhu al-hajj) until the day of sacrifice (yam al-nahar, also called yam al-adha or 'Id al-adha—the Festival of Sacrifice), which is celebrated by Muslims all over the world until our time. Islam has also adopted the Abrahamic (Ibrahimi) ritual of stoning the jamarat (stoned-satans), at Mina on the 10th day of Dhu al-hajj. Here is an interesting feature of the hajj: During the state of ihram, the pilgrims are forbidden not only from destroying any life, not even a blade of grass, but also from engaging in sexual life and even from cutting hair and nails. Interestingly, this was a feature of the pre-Islamic asceticism, but still continues in Islamic pilgrimage (61). It should be mentioned here that Islam has also adopted the pre-Islamic conception of the haram (forbidden) territory where the holy places of divinities were surrounded by protected lands on which the beasts which were consecrated to them grazed in peace. Muslim pilgrimage also includes the pre-Islamic custom of sa'y (running) between Safa and Marwa hills in celebration of Hagar's running between these two hills looking for water (whence comes the story of the miracle well Zamzam) "or rather following an old ambulatory rite" (62)

At any rate, although Islam has adopted some features from the pagan Arab hajj, still the fact remains that it has introduced some new features in order to suit its purposes. These include the halt on the plains of "Arafat going to Muzdalifa on the way to Mina to make sacrifice, and tahlil (de-sanctification) which begins only after the 'Umra (lesser hajj) is completed at Mecca, and followed by the head shaving, nail cutting, and at last, taking the bath/shower (ghusl) (63).

We have seen above the roots of the hajj in Islam with both the Pagan Arab and Hebrew/Jewish, tradition, particularly with that of Ibrahim (cf. Q. 3. 95, 97). However, Allah has granted some concessions for particular cases.

To begin with, if an ahl-i-nisab is incapable of performing the hajj personally because of physical or mental problems, or even the transportation problem for a non-local Muslim, and for a woman, want of an eligible male companion (husband or a relative—dhu mahram, that is, a person with whom her marriage is unlawful), he/she must send a naib (male, adult representative) to perform the pilgrimage on his/her behalf; (naib-i-haji is one who either has already completed his obligatory hajj himself or not an ahl-i-nisab). By the way, this naib cannot perform hajj for more than two absentees (ma'dhur) at one time.

In addition to what is discussed above, there are other concessions granted by Allah for emergency situations which clearly show what is called Islamic liberalism. To begin with, a person has arrived in Mecca but unfortunately is unable to perform the hajj because of unexpected physical or mental problem. To face this situation, the Qur'an says emphatically, "perform the pilgrimage and the visit (to Mecca) for Allah. And if ye are prevented, then send such gifts as can be obtained with ease, and shave not your heads until the gifts [sacrificial animals] have reached their destination. And whoever among you is sick or hath an ailment of the head must pay a ransom of fasting or alms-giving of offering [animal sacrifice]. And if ye are in safety, then whosoever contententh himself with the visit for the pilgrimage (shall give) such gifts as can be had with ease. And whosoever cannot find (such gifts), then a fast of three days while on the pilgrimage, and of seven when you have returned; that is, ten in all. That is for him whose folk are not present at the Inviolable Place of Worship . . ."(Q. 2. 196). It goes without saying that this is probably the most liberal provision granted by Allah even in a fundamental obligation. As for the sa'y (running), Allah has also allowed options in these words: "Lo! (the mountains) As-Safa and Al-Marwa are among the indications of Allah. It is, therefore, no sin for him who is on pilgrimage to the House (of God) or visiteth it, to go around them (as the pagan custom is). And he who doeth good of his own accord (for him), lo! Allah is responsive, Aware"(2.158).

Looking at another ceremony of the hajj at Mecca, viz. the tawaf (circumamubulation) of the ka'ba (Q. 3. 96f.; also cf. Ps. 26. 6; 27.

6), we again find both Jewish and Pagan Arab connections (64). In passing, it should be pointed out here that since the tawaf is not sanctioned by the Qur'an, it is not an obligatory rite, rather it is a sunnah established by the Prophet on his last pilgrimage ("Farewell Pilgrimage"—hajjat al wida'), who adopted from the pagan Arab "'umra". He also introduced some new elements: the tawaf al-qudum and the tawaf al-wada' (circumambulation of arrival and departure/ farewell respectively). There is also another interesting change in the course of the tawaf: The pagan Arab course (going around) used to have been clockwise: keeping the ka'ba on the right), whereas the Islamic tawaf is anti-clockwise. Another more fundamental reform Islam has introduced is the prohibition of the pre-Islamic practice of making the tawaf naked (cf. Q. 7. 31). In our present day, there is another unprecedented concession is to make tawaf on a wheelchair or even a stretcher, as the physical condition of a haji requires.

In this connection, we should mention other interesting concessions to sacrifice and stoning at Mina: One may choose any animal—goat or sheep or even join in a camel or cow sacrifice with six other hajis. The most liberal flexibility is granted in this. If a haji cannot go himself/herself personally, for some reasons, for both stoning and sacrifice, a naib (representative) can be delegated to perform these rites. Still another important concession is granted is that of a person who could not afford to perform the sacrifice, this can be compensated for by fasting (65).

Our discussions concerning the ritual of hajj has given us a clear idea that during that period the whole atmosphere becomes abnormal, some say "mystical" without any amusement of normal life. Notwithstanding that situation, Islam has declared 11th to 13th Dhu al-Hajj ayyam al-tashriq (days of eating, drinking and self-indulgence, which means, the life is out of the state of ihram). Notwithstanding the custom to spend these days at Mina, the Qur'an

(2. 203) has allowed an option: "Remember Allah through appointed days. Then whoso hasteneth (his departure) by two days, it is no sin for him, and whoso delayeth, it is no sin for him . . ."

To end this discussion on the institution of the hajj in Islam, let us say a few words about the well-known sermon (khutba) delivered by the Prophet (well-known as the khutba al wada'—Farewell Sermon) on the occasion of his hajjat al-wada' (Farewell Pilgrimage) in 632 C. E. (the year of his death). To begin with, according to popular judgment, this was his most comprehensive sermon (happened to be the last) dealing not only with matters relating to the individual and the community, but also clarifying the universal character of Islam and its message, On that occasion of the hajj, the Islamic lunar calendar introduced, by abolishing the intercolation (cf. Q. 9. 36 f.).

It should be stated here that since the hajj cannot be performed alone or in a place other than Mecca, the prophetic message directly focused on the universality of the pilgrimage, a pan-Islamic annual reunion. So, the hajj jama'at (congregation) of our time is the largest annual religious gathering of this type in the world, bringing together millions of pilgrims of the Muslim community with different nationalities from every corner of the world. Interestingly, here in the hajj congregation all Muslims—black and white, yellow and brown, kings and subjects and men and women are absolutely equal, and perform the obligations of the hajj rites shoulder to shoulder, without any sign of distinction whatsoever. In practice, it is the annual demonstration of the spirit of the Qur'anic verse 3. 103.

Finally, interestingly enough, Islam has not only integrated the pre-Islamic Arab practice of 'umra into its institution of al-Hajj but has also allowed the non-ahl-i-nisab Muslims to perform it only for merits (thawab). It is especially for this reason, that all Muslims—rich and poor—travel to Mecca round the year. Therefore, Islam has demonstrated its liberalism, dynamism and universalism by not disallowing the non-ahl-i-nisab Muslims from visiting the holiest places (Mecca and Madina) of their faith that they yearn all their lives.

CHAPTER 3 : References

1. Cf. Q. 13. 4; 29. 61, 63; 31. 25; 39. 38; 10. 23; 16. 53; 29. 65; 6. 110; 16. 38; 35. 42; 6. 137.
2. Q. 7. 180; 17. 110; 20. 8; 59. 24.
3. Cf. Q. 3. 26 f.; 59. 24.
4. Ethico-Religious Concept in the Qur'an, McGill University Institute of Islamic Studies, McGill University Press, Montreal, 1966, P. 65, ref. to Ibn Ishaq, 1, 28.
5. Islam, Weidenfeld and Nicolson, London, 1966, p. 32.
6. Ibid.
7. Ibid., p. 34.
8. Ibid., pp. 33f.
9. D. B. Macdonald, "Djinn", Shorter Encyclopaedia of Islam (SEI); Q. 37. 158.
10. D. B. Macdonald, "Allah", (SEI).
11. Ibid.
12. For more information about the remaining beautiful names of Allah, cf. "Allah", op. cit., especially Q. 59. 22ff.
13. Q. 20. 114; 22. 6, 62; 24. 25; 31. 30.
14. Macdonald, op. cit., Allah is also the Shaper (Al-Musawwir: Q. 59. 24; the Beginner (Al-Mubadi); the Restorer (Al-Mu'id: Q. 29. 19; 85. 13); the Giver of Life (Al-Muhyi: Q. 41. 39); the Sender of the dead from the graves (Al-Ba'ith); the Assembler of all again, at the Last Day (Al-jami': Q. 3. 9; 4. 140); the Guardian (Al-Hafiz: Q. 86. 4); the King and the Lord of Kingship (Malik Al-Mulk": Q. 3. 26); the Governor (Al-Wali: Q. 13. 11); the Preventer (Al-Muqtadir: Q. 18. 45); the Tyrant (Al-Jabbar: Q. 59. 23).

15. "Allah" op. cit.; also cf. Q. 13. 27; 16. 93; 74. 31.

16. Buhl, op. cit., ref. Q. 26. 195 sq.

17. In the following order: (1) Psalms (Jabbur) to David, (Dawud), (2) Law (Torah) to Moses (Musa), (3) Gospel (Injil) to Jesus ('Isa), Qur'an to Muhammad Q. 3. 3; 4. 163; 5. 66; 17. 55; 61. 6.

18. Aside from the Prophet Muhammad, there are as many as 27 well-known Semitic messengers named in the Qur'an. They are referred to as being Muslims too, in a literary sense, of course: Adam (as well as his wife, Eve and their two sons Aable and Cain), Idris (Enoch), Nuh (Noah, the ark and the flood), Hud, SalihIbraham (Abraham), Isma'il (Ishmael), Ishaq (Isaac), Lut (Lot), Luqman, Ya'qub (Jacob), Yusuf (Joseph), Shu'aib (Shaab), Ayyub (Job), Musa (Moses), Harun (Aron), Dhu'l Kifl (Ezekiel), 'Imran, Dawud (David), Sulayman (Solomon and his relation with the Queen Sheba), 'Ilias (Elias), Al-Yasa'(Elisha), Yunus (Jonah), Zakariyya (Zechariah), Yahya (John the Baptist), and 'Isa (Jesus and his 12 disciples), and Mariyam (Mary, the mother of Jesus).

19. They are A'ad; Kahaf and Raqim; Jalut (Goliath), Talut; Dhu'l-Kifl; Pha'un (Paraaoh); Yajuj and Majuj;(Gog and Magog); Haman; Sabi'in (Sabaian); Majuj (Magian); Ar-Rum (Romans); Thamud; Saba' (Sheba); The Twelve Tribes of Israel that travelled with Moses; Tubba'in (Tobba); and Madyan (Midian).

20. The Suras are: Al-'Imran (The Family of 'Imran: 3); Al-Ma'dah (The Table Spread: 5); Yunus: 10; Hud: 11; Yyusuf (Joseph: 12); Ibrahim (Abraham : 14); Bani 'Israil (The Children of Israel: 17); Maryam (Mary: 19); Al-Anbia (The Prophets: 21); Al-Namal (The Ant: 27); Al-Qasas (The Stone: 28); Ar-Rum (The Romans: 30); Luqman : 31); Saba (Sheba : 34); Al-Mu'men (The Believer: 49); Nuh (Noah: 71).

21. Stewart, P. S., Unfolding Islam, 1ˢᵗ. ed., Ithaca Press, U. K., 1994, p. 59. For the remaining Semitic messengers, cf. n. 24 above.

22. <u>Op. cit.</u>, p. 30.
23. <u>Ibid.</u>, p. 32.
24. <u>Op. cit.</u>, p. 35; also cf. A. J. Wensinck, "Iblis", <u>SEI</u>.
25. Schoeps, <u>op. cit.</u>, p. 245.
26. Cf. A. J. Wensinck, "Salat", <u>SEI</u>. The English word "prayer" is equivalent to the Arabic word <u>du'a</u> (which means expression of gratitude or thanks-giving to God (Allah), in a religious context, or to a patron in a secular sense).
27. Cf. Q. 5. 6; Th. W. Juynball, "Ghusl", <u>SEI</u>; J. Schacht, "Wadu", <u>SEI</u>; A. S. Tritton, "Tahara", <u>SEI</u>; also cf. "kitab al-Tahara" in <u>Hadith</u>, <u>Bukhari</u> and <u>Muslim</u>.
28. Also cf. A. J. Wensinck, "Tayammum", <u>SEI</u>.
29. Cf. "<u>Kitab/Bab al-Salat</u>" in <u>Bukhari</u> and <u>Muslim</u>; also cf. A. J. Wensinck, <u>op. cit.</u>, "Salat", <u>SEI</u>
30. According to one opinion, if a person is away from home, for a distance of at least 45 miles or 72 hours, he/she is allowed to perform <u>qasar</u> prayer. But we have to consider the means and condition of travelling in the 9th and 10th centuries when the <u>Shari'a</u> was in the process of being codified, when the travelling was either on foot or at best on camel; and the travelling means at our time. The <u>qada</u> (belated) is also allowed under the same circumstances.
31. Cf. Anonymous, "<u>haid</u>", <u>SEI</u>; anonymous, "nifas", <u>SEI</u>. It may be mentioned that for the <u>haid</u> the period depends on individual woman's habit, but maximum is 7 days; as to the <u>nifas</u>, 30 days is for all women (Cf. Q. 2. 222).
32. Cf. Q. 70. 23; 74. 43; 75. 31; 107. 5; 108. 2.
33. Cf. B. Schriek, "Isra", <u>SEI</u>; J. Horovitz, "Mi'raj", <u>SEI.</u>
34. Cf. "<u>Salat,op. cit.</u>; also cf. Q. 14. 37; 19. 31; 20. 132; 21. 73.
35. Cf. "Islamism et Persisme", <u>Revue de l' Histoire des Religions</u> (<u>R H R</u>), (1901), XL111, 15.

36. For complete information concerning names and times of the five daily prayers, cf. A. J. Wensinck, "Mikat", SEI; Muslim, "Masajid", h. 228f.; al-Nas'I, "Mawaqit", bab 23.

37. Also cf. Th. W. Joynboll, "Djum'a", SEI.

38. Ibid.

39. Gaudefroy-Demombynes, M., Muslim Institutions, trns. From French by J. P. MacGregor, London, George Allen & Unwin LTD, 4th impression, 1968, p. 102.

40. "Sawm", op, cit.

41. G-Demombynes, op. cit., p. 102.

42. Cf. M. Plessner, "Ramadan", SEI.

43. Cf. also al-Bukhari, "Sawm", bab 15.

44. For complete information concerning fasting and all related rites governing it, cf. "Sawm", op. cit.

45. Hedayetullah, Muhammad, Dynamics of Islam: An Exposition, Trafford, Victoria, B. C., 2002, p.67.

46. "Zakat", SEI.

47. Ibid.

48. Op.cit., P. 105.

49. Ibid., also cf. T. H. Weir, "Sadaka", SEI.

50. For specific information on this subject, cf. "Zakat", op. cit.; G-Demombynes, op. cit., p. 105. There is also a Zakat on life, called the zakat al-fitr (alms given on the occasion of the 'Id al-Fitr (the festival following the Fast of Ramadan).

51. Cf. 9. 58 ff.; 2. 195, 215, 219, 261-65, 271-74; 3. 92; 4. 114; 25. 67; 58. 12; 63. 10; 64. 16; 65. 7.

52. Ibn Ishaq, Sirat . . . , 1, 266.

53. Muruwwa means virtues such as generosity and bravery, patience, and trustworthiness and truthfulness. Prophet Muhammad was gifted with these virtues, as is well-known. Muslims adopted in their lives these pagan Arab qualities. (cf. Stewart, op. cit., p. 21).

54. Izutsu, op. cit.,p. 76.

55. Ibid., p. 77.

56. Ibid., p. 78; also cf. Q. 25. 67.
57. Op. cit., p. 81, also cf. pp. 81-88; for conditions requiring to perform the hajj, cf. Q. 22. 25ff. For complete information on the pilgrimage, cf. A. J. Wensinck, "Hadjdj", SEI.
58. "Hadjdj", op. cit.; also cf. F. Buhl, "Tawaf", SEI; Ibn Hisham, Sirat . . . , 1, 51; Smith, W. Robertson, Religion of the Semites: The Fundamental Institutions, Schocken Books, New York, 1972, p. 321.
59. Cf. Exd. 19. 19, 10, 14; 11. 15; "Hajj", op. cit.
60. Cf. I. Goldziher, "Revue de l' Histoire des Religious", (R H R), xxxv11, 318, 320f.; also cf. Q. 2. 197.
61. Cf. G-Demombyne, op. cit., p. 86.
62. For complete information about the remaining ceremonies of the hajj, cf. Ibid., pp. 89ff.; "Hadjdj", op. cit.; R. Parel, "Umra", SEI; Ibn Hisham, op. cit., 1, pp. 70 ff.; also cf. Q. 2. 198, 203.
63. Cf. "Tawaf", op. cit,; Ps. 366; Ibn Hisham, op. cit,. 1, 52, 820.
64. To remember, head-shaving is also nonobligatory, and there is no time legally prescribed for the sacrifice, but the two other rites are limited to the 10th of Dhu al-Hajj.
65. Cf. the article "Hajj", SEI.

CHAPTER 4

THE SHARI'AH (The Legal System)

The word shari'ah(shar'a) means the "path or the road leading to the watering place", that is, a way to be followed to the source of life. As a technical term, it means the Canon Law of Islam. "The most important and comprehensive concept for describing Islam as a function is the concept of the Shari'a or shar'" (1).

Shari'ah (jurisprudence) is considered to be the most comprehensive system that the Muslim jurists (fuqaha) developed for the Muslims to follow in their everyday life. It is a continuation of the Jewish system called Halakha, and the literature for the system is Talmud in Judaism and Fiqh in Islam. The people who developed the whole system and its literature in the Jewish system are rabbis and their equal in Islam are 'ulama' (sing. 'alim: scholars in religion in both systems, but not priests).

There are four schools of jurisprudence which reflect the four different interpretations of the Qur'an and the hadith (sunna).That means, a Muslim can follow any one of them fully or all of them partly in his/her daily life without violating basic principles Islam. This is a good example of liberalism of the shari'ah or Islam.

In passing, it should be stated here that the technical use of the word shari'ah is established by the Qur'an. For example, "Then We gave thee (O Muhammad) a Shari'ah [a clear road] of Our commandment; so follow it and do not follow the lusts of those who do not know (454. 18); "He hath enjoined on you (<u>Shari'ah</u>) the religion which Commanded unto Noah, and that which We inspire in thee (Muhammad), and that which Commanded unto Abraham and Moses and Jesus, saying: Establish the religion and be not divided therein . . ."(42. 13). "And unto thee have We revealed the Scripture with the truth, confirming whatever Scripture was before it, and watcher over it. So judge between them by that which Allah hath revealed, and follow not their desires away from the truth which hath come unto thee. For each, We have appointed a divine law and a traced-out way (a <u>sharia'</u> and a <u>minhaj</u>) . . ." (5. 48). Commenting on the above-mentioned passages relating to the Shari'a, Dr. Fazlur Rahman says: "In its religious usage, from the earliest period, it has meant the 'highway of good life, i. c, religious values expressed functionally and in concrete terms" (2).

Regarding the areas and the application of the <u>shari'ah</u>, Joseph Schacht says: "The <u>shari'ah</u>, as <u>forum externum</u>, regulates only the external relations of the subject to Allah and His fellow-men and ignores his inner consciousness, his attitude of the forum internum" (3). According to this writer, the <u>shari'ah</u> demands and is only deals with the fulfillment of the prescribed laws or rules. It means that although the <u>shari'ah</u> is taken to be the most elaborate code of Muslim life, still it is not a kind of "truncated" set of regulations and laws, since it does not have any jurisdiction over a Muslim's internal life, like <u>niya</u> (intention) which is needed for many religious rites, even though it does not require any impulse from the heart. There is a controversy about the jurisdiction of the <u>Shari'ah</u> among the different schools of Muslim jurisprudence especially Mu'tazilites. According to the orthodox view, the <u>Shari'ah</u> is the basis (<u>mansha'</u>) for the judgement of actions as good or bad, which can only come from Allah, whereas, according to the Mu'tazilites, it only confirms the verdict of intelligence which has preceded it. Notwithstanding, Dr. Fazlur Rahman views the <u>Shari'a's</u> jurisdiction from another angle—the Din, the Way: "Shari'a is the following or application of that Way in Muslim life. It is in this correlative sense that the Qur'an says: God 'hath ordained for you a Way to be followed', and again 'Do they, have any partners of God who have ordained for them the path to be followed'" (42. 13, 21) (4). Thus, the Shari'ah and Din are coterminous. However, notwithstanding the technical differences, for the Muslims, who has submitted to the will of Allah, the main task is to explain and implement the Shari'ah—the Way or the Command of God. Therefore, being the complete code of Muslim life, the Shari'ah's jurisdiction "encompasses" the whole life of a practicing Muslim-religious, social-economic, legal, political and ethical. For these reasons, the Shari'ah is a complete code of a practicing Muslim.

Before closing this issue, let us say a few words about the Shari'ah vis-a-vis the Sufis: According to them, the law is only a starting point on the path of the Sufis: "On the one hand, it can be regarded as an indispensable basis for the further religious life, by which the fulfillment of the law has to be refined (shari'ah and haqiqa the 'mystical reality', then form a correlated pair); on the other hand, only as a symbolic parable and allegory, finally even as superfluous formalism which one has to cast off entirely". To the orthodox, "on the whole, the shari'ah is the most characteristic phenomenon of Islamic thought and forms the nucleus of Islam itself"(5). However, the real significance of the Shari'ah lies in the flexibility that it allows to its followers in their everyday practical life to follow provisions of either only one school of jurisprudence for all purposes or those of different schools for different purposes, without being guilty of any wrongful violation (sins), and there has never been any serious confrontation among the authorities of those schools of jurisprudence (madhahibs) since the beginning of the function during 9th and 10th centuries C. E.

Sources of the Shari'ah

To begin with, the Qur'an—the divine Word—is the number one source of the <u>Shari'ah</u>. That means, a Muslim must follow in his/her daily life what is ordained by Allah without any questions. In reality, there are some inconsistencies which are nothing but the reflections of the progressive nature of the Islamic system; the Qur'an had been revealed during a period of 23 years of the Prophet Muhammad's prophetic life, and it is well known that there are changes and flexibilities that Allah has brought down in some cases by the method of <u>al-nasik wa al-mansuk</u> (abrogater and abrogated: Cf. Q. 16. 101). In addition to the Qur'an, old Arab customs and practices are also included, <u>mutatis mutandis</u>, in the formation of the <u>Shari'ah</u>. Hence, Schacht says, "As to the material sources of Islamic law, many elements of widely differing derivation (e. g. Beduin ideas; commercial law of the trading town Mecca; agrarian law of the oasis of Madina, customary law of the conquered countries, some of it of Roman provincial origin; Jewish law) have been unhesitatingly retained and adopted" (6)

<u>Sunnah</u>: During the lifetime of the Prophet Muhammad, both the Qur'an and his acts and sayings (<u>sunnah</u>: practices, customs, sayings and his approval of others' actions), had provided guidance for the <u>Umma</u>. It should be mentioned that the Prophet's <u>sunnah</u> was a combination of both Arab and his personal acts (<u>sunan</u> pl. of <u>sunnah</u>). However, after his death, even though the Qur'an was there to guide the Muslims' life in general, but the Prophet's <u>sunnah</u> was missing. And within a few years after his death, the Muslim world spread quickly, first through conquests, then by the <u>Sufi</u> preaching.

However, for the administration of this vast empire, particularly the non-Arab parts, the Qur'an has not provided either no law at all, or laws inadequate to deal with many cases. Under those circumstances, the Muslim governments of the three khulafa-i-rashedin ('Umr, 'Uthman and 'Ali) who succeeded the Prophet after the first khalifa (Caliph), Abu Bakr, had no guide to administer the newly conquered territories especially where the Qur'an contained no rules except only their interpretation of the Prophet's sunnah where this was possible. Hence, for more than a hundred years after the Prophet's death, the Muslim governments left at least the civil administration of the empire to the local people, including Hindus in the subcontinent of today's Bangladesh, India and Pakistan, who had already been engaged in that job before the Muslim conquest. Hence, until the shari'ah had been codified, the Muslim administration had remained as "heterogeneous" as it was at the time of the conquest. After all those difficult days passed, some sensible persons began a career of collecting the Prophet's doings, sayings, and his approvals of others' actions (hadiths) (7). The total result of their collections was the codification of the six "canonical" collections (siha sitta) named after their collectors. The work of hadith collection undoubtedly had been a gruesome task for both the collectors and 8th century reporters. By the way, there were some "spurious" hadith, but these were related only in good faith. Referring to those hadiths, G-Demombynes says, "No doubt many of them are apocryphal and were invented in the 8th century in order to justify innovations and tendencies which were very foreign to the intentions of the Prophet" (8). Finally, hadith, being the oral tradition, has had the same problems as other such traditions as far as historicity and authenticity are concerned. Nevertheless, the hadith is the most important source of information, after the Qur'an, for making the Shari'ah.

(3)Ijma' (Consensus): After the Qur'an was already in existence, and the Hadith was now codified, the jurists set to codify the shari'ah by adding two other elements, namely, ijma' and qiyas. The reason for this was that although the hadith-collectors tried to bring some kind of order to their collections, the Qur'an and the commentators [tafsir], and sunna and commentaries, constituted a mass of material to make capital out of, rather than an epitome of principles and rules of conduct (9).

Under those circumstances, before arriving at consensus, two other minor but important elements, viz., ra'y (personal opinion) and ijtihad (personal interpretation) had to be used. In other words, when a particular case was not covered by Qur'an and the hadith, and the jurists could not come to a conclusion about it, then they applied their consensus, which definitely not that of the whole ummmah, to bring that particular case to the jurisdiction of the Shari'ah. The other objective for using ijma' was to ensure permanence and stability to the Shari'ah since it had passed through controversies throughout its formative stages. But, contrary to good intent, it became rigid. It was primarily because of this rigidity that during the medieval period, the secular authorities took action to produce a body of secular laws as the "qanun" which sometimes added, and often even "supplanted", the shari'ah.

4. Qiyas: (Analogical Deduction): Notwithstanding fuqahas' use of the three above-mentioned sources, there were still some cases not covered by those sources, and then the jurists proceeded another step further to use the qiyas. This source of the shari'ah allows a jurist to apply to a new case made to fit analogous cases. "And still later, some [Hanafi] jurists [in particular] used even more liberal and humanitarian principles, like istislah (public well-being) in considering a case and consequently pronouncing their fatwa (legal opinion"). (10). Commenting on the above-mentioned juridical technique, one writer says, "In this way, some remnant of the inductive, human input that characterized the actual method of the law schools in their attempt to realize the Shari'a's primary concern with human welfare, justice and equality, were acknowledged" (11).

As we have examined above, after a long process during which the fuqaha not only used the already known sources (e. g. the Qur'an and the hadith), they also developed some new ideas and mechanisms by applying their liberal policies in completing the codification of the shari'ah. Hence, M. W. Watt says, "The formation or codification of the Shari'ah (law) under the 'Abbasids was a testimony of their utmost regard for a universal law that covers what is in the Qur'an and what is told by the Prophet (Hadith, Sunnah), plus jurists' analogical deduction (Qiyas) and consensus (Ijma')"(12). However, at last, the 'Abbasid-fuqaha put their seal on the shari'ah qualifying it as "Infallible" which was totally unjustified for the simple reason that of the four sources of the shari'ah, only the divine decree (the Qur'an) is infallible, and not the other three sources—the human elements. It may be stated here that the question of the "infallibility" of the shari'ah has been a headache for the Muslim Umma since its codification: "The only possible justification that can be put forward to defend the theory of "Infallibility" of the Shari'ah was that it was intended to achieve unity and some sort of homogeneity in a vast vibrant and volatile multi-cultural, multi-religious, and multi-ethnic Muslim Community-Empire. The non-Muslim subjects of the Empire were conclusively affirmed as the dhimmis and the payment of the jizya for their protection was imposed"(13).

It may be pointed out here that because of the juridical differences in interpretations, the fuqaha established four schools of jurisprudence, such as the Hanafi School (d. 767), Shafi'I School (d. 820), Maliki School (d. 795), and Hambali School (d.855), named after the principal faqi (jurist). Commenting on the majahab (schools) and their interrelationships, vis-a-vis the government, G-Demombynes says, "The schools of law, founded in the 9th century on the orthodox basis, have maintained their differences until this day; they share among themselves the government of the orthodox Muslim world". "Their differences", continues the same author, "manifested in their mental attitudes, have a real political importance; but those madhahib (sing. Madhhab) are orthodox rites, not dissenting sects; a Muslim may pass from one of the four madhahib to another without committing a sin" (14). Here it should be emphasized that the differences are only in minor issues. It goes without saying that these juristic divisions provided further liberty to the Muslims to demonstrate the spirit of their tolerance and openness to one another even in an important matter like the shari'ah and its different schools (majahib), which the Muslims follow in their every day life with utmost tolerance.

The subject-matter of the shari'ah may be divided into arkan (sing. Rukn: 'ibadat-obligations like worship), mu'amalat (public matters: civil as well legal) and 'uqubat (punishment). In addition, it may be mentioned that from the beginning, a certain practical intent was part of concept by the shari'ah for it is The Way, conferred by Allah, wherein Muslims are to conduct their lives so that they can realize the Divine Will. However, according to Dr. Fazlur Rahman, ". . . it includes all behavior, spiritual, mental and physical. Thus, it comprehends both faith and practice: assent to or belief in One God is part of Shari'ah just as are the religious duties of prayer and fasting, etc."(15). Evidently, the inclusion of the inner behavior (spiritual and mental) within the jurisdiction of the shari'ah is only indirectly, as it is the Divine Will and 'Way' which is comprehensive, that is a total way of life. But the rulers of the shari'ah (quddat, sing. Qadi) can never bring someone to justice for only thinking of doing or planning to do, even the most terrible acts, e. g. killing, until and unless it is practically done. We, therefore, conclude that only the physical or external acts of a Muslim come within the jurisdiction of the shari'ah.

In order to understand the comprehensive areas of Muslim life that are covered by the shari'ah, let us deal with the list of activities (a'mal) that fall within the scope of the shari'ah as found in fiq which contains the complete information about the shari'ah. To begin with, this includes 'ibadat, mu'amilat and 'uqubat, as stated before. However, since these regulations are not of equal importance, they are further divided into five legal categories (al-ahkam al-khamsa): (1) what is obligatory (fard), what we must perform or otherwise will be punished for missing or neglecting to do. Further, a distinction is made between individual duty (fard 'ayn), e. g. ritual Prayers, Fasting, Pilgrimage, Zakat, and what is collective obligation (wajib or fard kifaya) which one can pass by if it is performed by other members of the family or even of the community, for instance, funeral prayers (salat al-janaza), the two 'Id prayers (salat al'Idyn) and jihad (fiting in the way of Allah with arms), (2)Sunnah (meritorious duties of two kinds), viz., muakkadah and ghayrmuakkada (emphasised and not emphasized responsibilities). In this category also included are mandub (recommended), mustahab (desirable), and nafl (voluntary actions), the performance of which is rewarded (thawab) but neglect of which is not punished. (3) Mubah/murakhas) indifferent actions, the performance or negligence of which the shari'ah leaves open, and for which there is neither reward nor punishment sanctioned. (4) Makruh (reprehensible) actions which are not punishable but only admonished. (5) Haram—(forbidden actions: punished here and hereafter) of which there are different categories, for instance, kabirah and saghirah (grave and venial sins, for instance, disbelief in Allah, killing, stealing, raping, etc, and cheating, lying, etc. respectively), and ta'addi (trespass) for which there is no punishment.

From the above discussion of the jurisdiction and scope of the shari'ah, it is clear that the practical character of the shari'ah is flexible, the fuqaha formulated it to be so; it is pragmatic relating to the actual life of the practising Muslims. As a matter of fact, it is abundantly clear that the shari'ah's flexible character is a reflection of what Islam is as a total system of Muslim life.

Remembering the theory of "infallibility" of the shari'ah, it may be emphasized that the final effect of the acceptance of the "Shafi'i school's formulation of the four main sources of the shari'ah, discussed above, effectively lead to a denial of the individual right to ijtihad, for this is incompatible with infallibility"(16). It is contrary to the spirit of flexibility, which the jurists played in the course of the codification of the shari'ah. Thus, a writer says, "Islamic law, the product of an essentially dynamic and creative process, now tended to become fixed and institutionalized". "While individual scholars like Ibn Taymiyya (d. 1328) and al-Suyuti (d.1505) demurred", continues the same writer, "the majority position resulted in traditional belief prohibiting substantive legal development. This is commonly referred to as the closing of the gate or door of ijtihad"(17). Unfortunately, in a liberal religious system like Islam, this kind of provision is contradictory. It led to what is called taqlid (blind following of tradition) which is completely against the Islamic principle of "creativity" which helped in the codification of the shari'ah.

The next extremely important stage in the process of the formation of the shari'ah was the rise of Sufism (Mysticism) as a different way (tariqa), a bit different from the shari'ah, the orthodox way. Since the rise of Sufism (first individually from the 8th century C. E. later in orderly or organized way from the 11th century) as a collective spiritual way, thus shari'ah and Tariqah ran parallel dividing the hitherto united Umma (18). Nevertheless, the famous Sufi-philosopher-theologian, al-Ghazzali (d. 1111), who felt division in the united Islamic body politic, tried to synthesise the "two ways". With that in mind, he wrote his famous work: Ihya' 'ulum al-din (Revivification of the Science of the Faith). In this work, inter alia, al-Ghazzali had said that both shari'ah and Tariqa are integral parts of Islam, and represent two branches of Islam—the exterior and interior respectively. Thus one cannot be completed without the other if a Muslim is to live a complete Islamic life—the former leads to the latter. Thus, commenting on the interrelationship between the shari'ah and the tariqa, one writer says: "Alongside the exterior path of law (shari'ah) is the interior path or way (tariqa of mysticism, . . . While the shari'ah provides the exoteric way of duties and rights to order the life of the individual and Community, the tariqa offered an esoteric path or spiritual discipline, a method by which Sufis sought not only to follow but to know God"(19). Al-Ghazzali did not like the kalam either. Therefore, in order "to integrate the Sufi method with the formulations of the kalam, he advocated the 'living through' or 'interiorization of purely rational beliefs . . .'" "This synthesis, worked out into a programme of inner, spiritual purification culminating in the single-minded love of God, he declared to be the true meaning of the shari'ah." "This inwardness of the faith, he called Din [execution of the shari'ah]. The Din is then the essence of the shari'ah, its inner life. The shari'ah without the Din is an empty shell and the Din without the shari'ah obviously cannot exist". Hence, Ghazzali's efforts may be described as a bilateral synthesis between kalam and Sufism, on the one hand, and sharia'h and Sufism on the other"(20).

Moreover, shari'ah, as the only unifying platform, has brought under its jurisdiction all the factional religious divisions in the Ummah. Thus, it is said: "The four major currents characterizing religious life in Islam and, to an ever increasing extent, dividing it among themselves from the 4th/10th century onward, viz. rationalism, Sufism, theology, and law, could only be synthesized and integrated under some comprehensive religious concept like that of the Shari'ah"(21).

Speaking about the jurisdiction of the Shari'ah, it should be stated emphatically that it is a comprehensive and synthetic body of laws which brings together within its jurisdiction the law of orthodoxy, the rational truth ('aql) of the philosophers and fuqaha (theologians), and the spiritual truth (haqiqah) of Sufism: "This inclusiveness points to a religion, that is, Islam, which is the foundation and source of the above-mentioned branches of authority in Islam" (22). It should be stated clearly that shari'ah and reason are not opposed to each other. In fact, the simple maxim is: "The Shari'ah is rational and the rational is the Shari'ah. In other words, Shari'ah and rationalism, being the two avenues of the knowledge, cannot of necessity be contradictory" (23).

It should also be stated that the orthodox Islam has branded or qualified the Shari'ah as "sacrosanct" and "infallible"; however, Muslim modernists have been challenging the traditional attribution, and thus the unchangeable authority of the Shari'ah, and they claim the right to reform in the light of modern ideas and needs of the society at large by exercising the right of ijtihad. This is, of course, reasonable because since the introduction of the fiqh, there has been no codification of the law in a modern way: "The several codifications of the last two centuries had been made under the influence of European ideas, e. g. in the Ottoman Empire, and for the use of non-specialists, and are not applied by any other Shari'ah law courts"(24).

Another issue that should also be stressed is that the shari'ah is a unifying force only in the matter that no other equivalent legal system was codified since then. Moreover, the above-mentioned divisions and classes of human actions that have been brought under the sphere of the shari'ah show much flexibility; the different majhab and different jurists within each school enjoyed themselves and allowed for others. This liberty of expression and interpretation that is rooted in the structure of the shari'ah makes the system of Islam one of the most liberal religious-social systems of the world.

In this context, Schacht says, "The reasons which lead to an action being classed under one of these categories may be of the most varied kinds and here that is a wide field for difference of opinion (ikhtilaf) among jurists. What one party considers absolutely forbidden or an absolute duty, the others often regard as reprehensible or meritorious in different ways. Here, however, the catholic tendency of Islam makes itself felt"(25). This certainly demonstrates the broadmindedness or openess to different opinions that the different schools and their respective fuqaha demonstrated even if this in regard to secondary matters. Eventually, since the establishment of the four majahib (schools), there have not been any more majhab established in the name of the shari'ah. By the way, it may be mentioned here in passing that the so-called Shi'ah-Sunni juridical differences only concern minor issues, as in the history of the four schools (majahib), and certainly not in major or fundamental matters.

Let us now say a few words about the administration and the application of the Shari'ah: In this connection, it should be mentioned clearly that since the codification of the Shari'ah, there was a kind of understanding between the 'ulama' and the government to the effect that the latter acknowledged the authority of the former enjoyed complete freedom of function, but in the case of a controversy, the latter issued independent regulations (qanun/siyasa) on legal matters and even established similar courts to administer these new regulations. This is yet another example of freedom the Muslims enjoy in legal matters. And to validate the ikhtilaf (controversy), they usualy cite a well-known hadith of the Prophet: "The differences of opinion within my community is a sign of the bounty (rahma) of Allah" (said the Prophet). In such a situation, it was accepted by all although theoretically Shari'ah's authority is accepted for all cases, but in practice, there are some exceptions. It is for this reason, especially, that certain actions had been characterised as "recommended" or "reprehensible". Further, a concession was granted to go around the rules of the Shari'ah by citing the popular theory of hila (necessity, which allows the breaking of the law).

Difference continued in practice as judges applied the laws of different majahib of Shari'ah in their courts. The motive force of the system continued as legal development and changes did take place when the 'ulamas' interpreted and sometimes clarified elaborate points of some clauses of the Shari'ah. In this matter, the contributions of the muftis (legal experts) were based on their understanding and interpretation of the clauses of the Shari'ah. During the subsequent times, these fatawa were collected and eventually became authoritative documents. This practice is still in use all over the Muslim world with some exceptions. In passing, it should be mentioned that the 'ulama' have been the guardians of the Shari'ah, as teachers, lawyers, judges and muftis. Nonetheless, they must not be misunderstood for priests; in fact, they are only teachers and experts in Shari'ah (Islamic law) and practice as the rabbis are.

Regarding the application of the Shari'ah, the 'ulama' played an important role: on the one hand, they were the administrators of the Shari'ah as the employees of the government, on the other hand, they were the ones who considered the Shari'ah as "impotent", that is, as not applicable in all cases or in all societies except in ideal Muslim society of the early time because of its being unchangeable. Therefore, to them Shari'ah is more of academic importance than it was useable for practical legal applications. This was not right because it was only their own narrow-minded understanding of the Shari'ah.

However, the early qadis announced their decisions applying their own right and putting their interpretations on the prescriptions of the Qur'an and the instruction of the khulafa, as well as on equity and on customary law. Thus, during the early Umayyad period the administration of justice made very important contributions to the development of the Shari'ah.

During the 'Abbasid period, the Shari'ah recognised the existence of the court of the nazir al-mazalim (grievance officer), to promote the regular administration and implementation of the Shari'ah and of the muhtasib (the office of the public morality in general). These ultimately became officially accepted institutions alongside the court of the Qadi. By the way, this court continues to function in some Arab countries like Saudi Arabia and Kuwait, and has recently been introduced in Pakistan and Iran. Hence, during the 'Abbasi period (750-1258) a twofold legal system became functional—the religious and the secular. Now, let us view the opinion of the modern-time Western scholar in Islamics regarding the pervasive nature of the Shari'ah: "The idealism of the law can be seen in the fact that the ethical categories such as recommended and reprehensible were not subject to civil penalties. Islamic law is also egalitarian; it transcends regional, family, tribal and ethical boundaries. It does not recognize social class or cast differences. All Muslims, Arab and non-Arab, rich and poor, black and white, caliph and craftsman, male and female, are bound by Islamic law as members of a single, transnational community or brotherhood of believers" (26).

It should be mentioned here that with the development and diversification of the social-political and economic conditions of the country, plus the regular growth of the trend of secularism, the non-religious authority exercise more authority in the legal system, e. g. in economical or financial and criminal matters, in international relations, constitutional affairs, war, etc. "To the jurisdiction of the Kadi, there was finally left only public worship and purely religious obligations, the law regarding marriage, family and inheritance, in part also pious foundations (waqf . . .), all fields which in the popular mind are more closely connected with religion, and in which the Shari'ah always prevailed" (27).

This is to be stated that the increase in the matters managed by the state resulted in an increase in the government's responsibility—in the legal matters. Nonetheless, the Shari'ah maintained its jurisdiction in those areas which had been under its jurisdiction since the beginning. However, although the Shari'ah lost its main patron in an empire, in the person of the 'Abbasid caliph in Baghdad in 1258, it reached its highest level as far as its jurisdiction was concerned in Istanbul, the headquarter of the Ottoman Empire, extending its authority as far as to Egypt, in the 16th and the 17th centuries, under the guardianship of the Ottoman Sultan-Khalifa. "Under the supreme-mufti (the shaykh al-Islam), the judges were orgaised in a hierarchical order. But, even then the criminal, financial and landed property laws which were secular laws and thus contrary to the Shari'ah, were governed by the temporal legislation called qanun-names"(28).

At any rate, the reform movement (tanzimat), "starting in the 19th century, introduced the codes, conceived on European lines, at first for the criminal, then for the panel law, but still as late as 1876 the civil law of the Shari'ah was codified in the Mecella (Arabic Majalla: book of law, like fiqh" (29). But that was outside the boundary of the Shari'ah tribunals.

The last attempt was made in 1926 when the Swiss civil and the Italian penal codes, which replaced the Shari'ah even for only religious laws like those relating to marriage, family and inheritance, were introduced. This was followed in 1928 by the omission of the last mention of the Shari'ah from the new Turkish constitution of 1924 which was the beginning of the total secularisation process (30). The only country where the Shari'ah had been officially abrogated by the introduction of atheism is Albania. The other country where the Shari'ah had been undergoing reforms is Egypt, since1883, when this country adopted the codes fashioned after the European model, but only to cover the issues abandoned by the Shari'ah in the course of the quick rise of secularism under Anglo-French influences; this process ended in 1931.

Although the increase in the affairs managed by the government resulted in an increase in the government's responsibilities in the legal field, yet the Shari'ah maintained its authority in those areas which had been under its jurisdiction since the beginning.

However, although the Shari'ah was no longer the principal code of law of the central government in a broken empire, in the person of the 'Abbasid Khalifah in Baghdad in 1258, it reached its highest position as far as its jurisdiction was concerned in Istanbul, the capital of the Ottoman Empire, extending its authority into Egypt, in the 16th and the 17th centuries, under the guardianship of the Ottoman Sultan-Caliphs. Under the supreme mufti (the Shaykh al-Islam), the judges were organised in a "hierarchical order". Nevertheless, even the criminal, financial and landed property laws which were secular and thus contrary to the Shari'ah, were governed by the temporal (non-religious) legislation called qanun-names.

The main focus of the aforesaid discussion has been on the scope and jurisdiction of the Shari'ah visa-a-vis the government and its administration. However, it is a different matter when we consider the position of the Shari'ah in common Muslim practices. Not withstanding all the facilities allowed by the Shari'ah itself, the Shari'ah occupies a special place in Muslim life as far as performance is concerned, a place filled with an emotional attachment which the awareness of religious obligation could have not created. Commenting on this, Schacht says, "Here it should always be remembered that there may be considerable differences in details in different periods and countries and that strictness and slackness in following the Shari'ah have nothing to do with tolerance or intolerance. Even in ritual and religious duties in the narrower sense, which mean most to Muslims, ignorance and gross neglect in general, but nevertheless throughout the whole Muslim world there is a striving to perform some at least of the main obligations as closely as possible. The usages especially, by which Muslims are externally distinguished from members of other creeds, are in general very closely observed and considered very important even if they are not according to the law, while, on the other hand, many religious obligations imperative in theory are quite neglected in practice. The law relating to marriage, family and inheritance is usually quite closely followed, but even here the Shari'ah is occasionally encroached upon by the local customary law ('ada, 'urf, desturi . . .)" (SEI).

As discussed earlier, Shari'ah is not only neglected from time to time in every day Muslim life, but sometimes it is misunderstood and thus misinterpreted. For example, the case of usury and interest (riba)which the pre-Islamic Arab money-lenders used to take from the borrowers who had to borrow under a difficult situation. The well-known case used to be like this: If a debtor who could not pay back the capital (money or goods borrowed) with the accumulated interest at the time it was due, he was given an extension of the time by which he had to pay, but at the same time the amount due was doubled. Reference is made to this in two verses of the Qur'an: "O ye who believe! Devour not usury, doubling and quadrupling (the sum lent). Observe your duty to Allah, that ye may be successful"(3. 130); "That which ye give in usury in order that it may increase on (other) people's property hath no increase with Allah; but that which ye give in charity, seeking Allah's countenance, hath increase manifold"(30. 39; also cf. 2. 275-80).

It may be pointed out that from all the passages of the Qur'an, it is clear that the prohibition of taking and giving interest did not refer to a business deal between creditor and the debtor, but only to a situation where the latter borrowed from the former for the latter's personal use.

Nonetheless, this case has been misinterpreted by the Muslims as a prohibition against paying or receiving interest on one's deposited money; of the other similar case is like this: Someone borrowed money from a bank to do business or take out a mortgage on some property. These two very common cases are absolutely different from those stated in the Qur'an where both taking and giving interest are strictly forbidden. Unlike the money lenders of the pre-Islamic Arab society, who were not the business partners of the debtors, the banks or financial institutions of our times are really in a way our business partners. They keep our money (our deposits) with which they do business, and in return, we receive a share of the profit. But there is a misnomer calling it "interest"; it should be called a business, as it is called in Pakistan. In the other case, when we borrow money from banks to invest either in the shares of these financial institutions (as bank shares or GIC), or to invest in other businesses, in both cases they are our business partners. The case of a mortgage is even more interesting: the debtor's home remains under the control of the creditor, and the bank can sell the home in case of default on the part of the debtor.

It should be stated here that according to the principles of nasikwa mansuk (Q. 16. 101), Islam is open to changes. Hence, some of the principles mentioned in the Shari'ah can be adjusted without the Qur'anic support, in consideration of the present-day circumstances. However, those problems should be dealt with piecemeal, rather than en masse. Shari'ah is not "infallible", as we have already mentioned. The energetic and dynamic Islamic civilization stayed behind when the once dormant Europe went ahead following the Renaissance, leaving the Islamic civilization, "once the jolter of Europe".

It should be stated clearly that the Shari'ah made dogmatic by some irrational jurists, for it would not allow the umma to bring about changes to go along with the scientific-technological progress. For instance, in Egypt, one of the most modern Muslim countries, which has been developing under Western (Anglo-French) influences for more than two hundred years, Muslims (mullas) wanted to make the Shari'ah the source of all laws in Egypt. As a result, desert law was introduced in parliament in 1977; then the Sadat government would have enforced the death sentence for renunciation of Islam. However, an opposition to that draft came from the Copts, particularly from those who had married Muslims and had become nominally Muslims themselves. After that draft was withdrawn in 1980, President Sadat declared the basic principle: "No politics in religion, no religion in politics"(32). For sure, this edict alarmed all religious peoples for it was against established Islamic tradition. Muslims opposed to the edict assassinated Sadat the following year. "The Muslim Brotherhood", the guardians of the Islamic orthodoxy in Egypt, "opposed not only this decree but also were against any measure aiming at freeing women, and asked for measures for sexual segregation. They also opposed the law that granted wives the right to initiate divorce" (33).

It should be stated here that in contradistinction to Egypt, Sa'udi Arabia, the religious home of Islam or Muslims, is the most traditional Muslim country, still both the Shari'ah and modernism have been functioning quite easily to make it one of the richest countries of the world, especially being the number one for producing oil. Commenting on Islamic liberalism in Saudi Arabia, Stoddard says, "Saudi Arabia is at once the most Muslim and the most Arab [Islamic] of [Muslim] countries. Its traditional, ethno-religious homogeneity, however, has included social and cultural diversity. Foreign forces of economic modernization, now challenge the values on which Saudi society and government has rested at the centre of the Arab and Islamic worlds" (34).

It is worth mentioning that the origin and development of today's Saudi Arabia beginning from the 18th century, bear witness of working of both tribal and Islamic forces side by side. As a matter of fact, the collaboration between a political ruler and a religious reformer, namely, Muhammad ibn Sa'ud and Muhammad ibn 'Abdul Wahhab respectively, laid the basis of today's kingdom of Sa'udi Arabia where the forces of modernism and religion have been working together in an unprecedented way. Abdul Wahhab, the leader of the Wahhabi movement, delivered the message of the original or traditional Islam by renouncing and later adding and stressing the unqualified unity of Allah, the Qur'an and the Sunnah (way of the Prophet Muhammad: tariqa-i-Muhammadiyah). As a matter of fact, it is a kind of neo-Sufi movement which gradually spread to other regions of the Muslim world, especially to the subcontinent of present day's Bangladesh, India and Pakistan (35). The union of "sword and faith" (religion and secularism) was unquestionably a practical example of Islamic liberalism where the two expressions of Islamic life are by no way in disagreement with each other, but in fact are complimentary to each other. This is the famous truth or fact in Islam-religion and secularism are not two "antagonistic forces" but in fact two forces are functioning together which has promoted liberalism and rationalism in Islam. In fact, in the present-day Saudi Arabia, over a million non-Arab workers from all over the world, especially from the West, work in oil and other industries; nevertheless, the Arab Bedouin culture and present-day Islam live and function hand-in-hand to provide the ruling Saudis with a moderate legitimising force.

In addition to being the World headquarters for oil industry, Saudi Arabia is also the home of Islamic holy places—Mecca and Madina which bring from all over the world, annually at the time of the hajj, millions of pilgrims from all over the world of different nationalities which offers particularly the Hijaj a more global feature than other parts of that country. Notwithstanding this event, it is yet counted as the most conservative Muslim country in the world. "Because of these characteristics, Saudi Arabia had developed the most practical and accommodating administrative apparatus for the Hijaj in particular" (36).

In addition, this system together with Wahhabism, developed a special type of administrative feature in the Hajj. Hence, "Acknowledgment of the Koran [sic] and the other sources of the shari'ah as the nation's constitution was a shrewd way in which to confirm Islamic legitimacy, and to leave open specific questions about how to deal with contemporary issues which were unanticipated by the early Muslim community" (37). By doing that, the Saudi governments have been logical in justifying the fresh elements vis-a-vis Islam and getting 'ulama's support on their side. That move helped the Saudi governments to go forward with the modernizing process without any problem to make the fundamentalist Islamic charter of the country. The Saudi governments had been successful in showing that modernism and Islamic orthodoxy are not opposed to each other in day-to-day life. "Saudi governments' rational and flexible policies in accommodating and promoting both Islamic and secular ideas are now well-known all over the Muslim world, and there has not been any opposition to or criticism of this reconciliation" (38) As a matter of fact, some advance the idea that Saudi governments had been propagating or transmitting Islamic message of liberalism promoting the solidarity of Muslim countries through many means especially by holding of many "Islamic

Summit conferences and hosting the OIC (Organisation of Islamic Conference"(39).

In concluding our discussion about the Shari'ah's liberalism and flexibility, we can say with confidence that the Shari'ah is quite flexible and modern if we only understand it properly with an open or liberal mind. Thus a writer says, "Throughout history, Islamic law has remained central to Muslim identity and practices, for it constitutes the ideal social blueprint for the 'good society'. The Shari'ah has been a source of law and moral guidance, the basis for both law and ethics. Despite vast cultural differences, Islamic law has provided an underlying sense of identity, a common code of behavior, for Muslim societies. As a result, in the past and again today, the role of Islamic law in Muslim society has been a central issue for the community of believers" (40).

CHAPTER 4 : References

1. Fazlur Rahman, Islam, Weidenfeld and Nicolson, London, 1966, p. 100.
2. Ibid. For more information about thee Shari'ah, cf. ibid., pp. 100-116; also see Gaudefroy-Demombines, M., Muslim Institutions, tr. J. P. Macgregor, London, George Allen & Unwin LTD., pp. 64ff.; J. Schacht, "Shari'a, SEI; Esposito, John L., Islam: The Straight Path, New York, Oxford University Press, 1988, pp. 75ff.
3. Op. cit.
4. Op. cit., p.100.
5. Schacht, op. cit.
6. Ibid.
7. For a brief history of "Hadith", cf. Th. W. Yuynball, SEI; also cf. G-Demombines, op. cit., pp. 6ff.; Esposito, op. cit., pp. 80ff.
8. Op. cit., p. 65.
9. Ibid., p. 66.
10. Hedayetullah, Muhammad, Dynamics of Islam: An Exposition, Trafford, Victoria, Canada, 2002, p. 144.
11. Esposito, op. cit., p. 84.
12. What is Islam, Longmens Green and Company, London, 1968, p. 123.
13. Hedayetullah, op. cit., p. 145.
14. op. cit., p. 67.
15. op. cit., p. 101.
16. Hedayetullah, op. cit., p. 148.
17. Esposito, op. cit., p. 85.

18. For a compact history of the rise of <u>Sufism</u> and its relations with the <u>Shari'ah</u>, cf. Fazlur Rahman, <u>op. cit.</u>, chs. 8 and 9, pp. 128-166; L. Massignon, "Tariqa", <u>SEI</u>.
19. Esposito, <u>op. cit.</u>, 103.
20. Fazlur Rahman, <u>op. cit.</u>, p. 106.
21. <u>Ibid.</u>, p. 109.
22. Hedayetullah, <u>op. cit.</u>, p. 152.
23. <u>Ibid.</u>
24. <u>Ibid.</u>, p. 153.
25. "Shari'ah", <u>Shorter Encyclopaedia of Islam</u>, <u>op. cit.</u>
26. Esposito, <u>op. cit.</u>, p. 89.
27. Schacht, <u>op. cit.</u>, <u>SEI</u>; also cf. W. Heffening, "Wakf", <u>SEI</u>.
28. Hedayetullah, <u>op. cit.</u>, p.159.
29. Berkes, Niyazi, <u>The Development of Secularism in Turkey</u>, McGill Institute of Islamic Studies, McGill University Press, Montreal, 1964, p. 168.
30. Cf. Smith, William C., <u>Islam in Modern History</u>, A Mentor Book, The New American Library, New York, 3rd. ed., 1963, p. 127. Constitution of the Republic of Turkey, Apr. 20, 1924, Art. 21.
31. For more information on this subject, cf. Schacht, "Riba", <u>SEI.</u>
32. Cf. Philip H. Stodard (ed.), <u>Change and the Muslim World</u>, Syracuse University Press, Syracuse, 1981, p. 57.
33. cf. <u>ibid.</u>
34. <u>op. cit.</u>, p. 137.
35. cf. Hedayetullah, M., <u>Sayyid Ahmad: A Study of the Religious Reform Movement of Sayyid Ahmad of Ra'e Bareli</u>, SH. Muhammad Ashraf, Lahore, 1st. ed., 197o, pp. 31, 95ff.
36. Hedayetullah, <u>Dynamics of Islam</u>, <u>op. cit.</u>, p. 167.
37. Stoddard, <u>op. cit.</u>, p. 139.
38. Hedayetullah, <u>Dynamics of Islam</u>, <u>op. cit.</u>, p. 168.
39. Cf. Stoddard, <u>op. cit.</u>, p. 139; also consult, Sunny, I., <u>The Organization of the Islamic Conference</u>, Pustaka Sinor-Harapan, Jakarta, 200.
40. Esposito, <u>op, cit.</u>, p. 75.

CHAPTER 5

Islamic/Muslim Family and Social Life

At the outset, it should be stated unequivocally that Muslim law derived from the Qur'an and Tradition (hadith) has not separated spiritual life from the temporal. This is in action throughout the whole Muslim world. However, sometimes it is contradicted by the local customs which occupy an important place in the actual lives of the Muslims. "It must also be remembered that the Arab-Muslim mind knows nothing of the custom of embodying principles in a formula of the manner of classical Roman law: the Qur'an and the Tradition have been called in to decide particular cases, and the Doctrine has, by analogy, extended to like cases the solutions which they offered" (1).

It should also be stated that the Muslim family was not a creation of the Prophet Muhammad. We are told that it is the original Arab family, placed within the structure of a higher religion. For the pre-Islamic Bedouin-Arab family, the important aspect of a life of plunder/pillage and a continuous fight to survive was the birth of many sons. This was assured by polygamy. The allocation of the sons was a highly important matter: a man's marriage to a girl of a different clan produced children. But during the life of the Prophet Muhammad, "the first kind of union was by far the most frequent in Arabia, as well as generally prevailing in the Eastern countries which the conquests brought into the Muslim Empire, and followed Romano-Byzantine of Semitic law" (2). To be sure, it is now a rule in the Muslim family.

The historical beginning of it is not easy to point out. However, some definite facts indicate that the customs or practices of married life were separate in Mecca and Madina, where they are said to have been influenced by the Jewish customs, and it is known that the marriage with the Meccan immigrants (mohajirin) were characterised by reluctance and often dispute. For good, the Prophet was successful in bringing this fashion into agreement or concord with benefits to both parties.

This is to be stated with emphasis that the Muslim family has been "patriarchal", and as the head of it, his (husband's) guardianship over his family-members, including the children even as adults down to their whole life, is unquestionable—an Abrahamic tradition. Accordingly, or naturally, the children of a family belong to their father, historically.

Here is another interesting fact of pre-Islamic Arab marriage which Islam has adopted: "In pre-Islamic days marriage was looked upon as a kind of sale in which, after the consent, of the parties had been given, the husband made to the wife's father a payment called mahr. Muslim marriage has kept this ancient form; but the dower is assigned to the wife and considered to be an indemnity for the sacrifice of her person" (3).

The marriage is usually arranged by a suitor. However, in order to refrain or void a refusal, the suitor obtains the positive opinion (yes); the suitor gets the green light and cooperation of an important person whose words and prestige will complete the day. It should be made clear that only when the financial matters (mahr/dowry) are settled or arranged between the two families, the date of the contract is fixed ('aqd-al-nikah). This brings to an end of the whole process of marriage. It should be emphasised that the consent of the two families is the number one condition essential for the validity of the marriage. A girl must give her consent only if she has reached the age of maturity, otherwise her father, if alive, or brother gives the consent, which the suitor declares. In the absence of a member of her family to give consent, a person appointed by the magistrate (hakim), will do that job.

In passing, the dowry (mahr) paid by the husband is allotted by the Qur'an to the wife, or her guardians (father/brother). It is also a common practice that the dowry may be paid two-thirds, to be paid at the time of the contact; the balance will be "after the consummation of the marriage and, still payable after a marriage has been broken" (4). To conclude this subject, it should be stated that "if the amount is not specified in the contract, it is fixed by resort to the mahr-al-mithl, a dowry of a value corresponding to the social rank of the wife" (5).

The marriage agreement has no particular religious nature. It may be celebrated in a mosque or at homes of the parties. The ceremony begins with the recitation of the sura Fatiha of the Qur'an, which is the introduction to every act in a Muslim's life. A khutba (admonition earnestly) is delivered by the wali of the bride, or by a mullah (learned person in Islam). "It is necessary also that the terms of contract will have grave moral and material consequences should be known to two persons, who will, in future, be able to bear witness to them; they are two 'udul . . . who have the name and qualifications which all witnesses to deeds must possess who are acceptable to the qadi" (6).

The marriage agreement may be made between two adult persons through their wali. The wali resolves the problem of uncertainties concerning the age in an arbitrary way and determines the consummation of the marriage as soon as both the marriage husband and wife have been recognised as having attained the age of maturity or puberty. By the way, an insane person may marry provided his <u>wali</u> assists with his presence.

Here is an important information: Muslim law has provisions forbidding the marriage of near relatives, including uncle and niece. However, a marriage between first cousins is sanctioned by custom. One can marry up to four wives separately or at any one time, and it is not allowed to marry two sisters. However, after the breakdown or dissolution of the marriage, either by the death of the wife or divorce, marriage with sister-in-law is allowed, as it was allowed in pre-Islamic Arabia (7).

It is important to know that marriage between a Muslim and non-Muslim is forbidden. The Qur'an had made an exception for the woman of the "tributaries" (<u>ahl al-kitab</u>), whom Muslims are permitted to marry (cf. Q. 2. 221, 235; 4. 3f., 25; forbidden degrees Cf. 4. 22ff.; 5. 5; 24. 32f.). (But the Shafi'I made such marriage impossible). In this respect, "the Qur'an permitted a woman to marry a man of a rank beneath her own only in exceptional circumstances; the status of the husband is determined by his rank in society, as well as by his fortune, which must be sufficient to ensure to his wife the continuation, materially, of her accustomed way of life. The husband is free to marry even a slave; the princes have always contracted unions with shepherdesses" (8).

In connection with the marriage, the whole occasion of ceremonies is called "'<u>urs</u>", and the spouses are "'<u>arus</u> and '<u>arusa</u>", beginning from the time of the agreement of the marriage contract, an act which is followed by a large feast (<u>walima</u>), which in reality celebrates the agreement of friendship or intimate association between the two families. All the members of their own social friends are invited.

"The doctrine makes it compulsory as being the essential public proclamation of the marriage. A refusal of the invitation is looked upon as an insult; the <u>qadi</u>, however, may not accept it" (9).

The most essential of customs related to the completion of the marriage is bathing. In the town, the bathing of the bride is the occasion of great merry-making among ladies. The embellishing of the bride, the evening when her hands and feet are dyed with henna (<u>laylat al-henna</u>), and her face beautified, is followed by another occasion for a feast which is held in the parent's house. Next day the wife is taken in procession to the husband's house where she is joyfully placed on a "throne" (stage), and the parents are set out—a third feast for the bride. In the meantime, the husband, having finished his bathing ceremony, goes to the mosque for a visit to a <u>qubba</u> of a saint, eventually returning home in a sort of procession with amusement (music with singing and dancing). There he is conducted into the presence of his wife. During those ceremonies, it is believed, that the bride and bridegroom are especially exposed to the attacks of the <u>jinns</u> and to the danger of the evil eye. At that time it is the responsibility of their guardians to protect them in their best way. "Various rites, in which <u>ears</u> of barley or of rice, pomegranates, almonds, fish and eggs play a part to save him from impotence and help to ensure the fertility of the bride" (10). Sometimes in some places a public demonstration is held to ensure her virginity. However, the difficulty of this formality has encouraged people, especially those who are directly involved in this wedding, to modify or cancel it totally. Consummation is followed by a feast of happiness. However, the period of seven days immediately following puts on both parties certain prohibitions which are seriously and honestly absorbed.

Another aspect of marriage is the relationship between the husband and the wife in all matters of family and social affairs. In this connection, the law and custom gave the husband absolute authority over his wife and the whole family. This is why the Qur'an says: "the man has a grade (authority) over woman"(2. 328). The Qur'anic law, quite favourable to the wife, thus gave her a status which is, in various ways, more advantageous than that bestowed even by modern Western countries. As for the financial matters, she retains her control, as a base, over the whole matters. Often she can keep her own estate; "she remains mistress of the dowry and of any goods she may acquire by inheritance, by gift, as the fruit of her own labour". "In practice", emphasises the learned author, "it is difficult for her to exercise those rights; but she is certain of maintenance, lodging and service, according to her rank"(11). Notwithstanding the aforesaid rights of the wife, the Qur'an says to their relations clearly, "women are your raiment for you and you are raiment for them" (hunna libasun lakum, wa antum libasun lahum" (2. 187).

It goes without saying that the husband is the guardian of his wife. Thus The Qur'an says, ". . . and men are a degree above them"(2. 228; 4. 34). This is called the guardianship—man takes care of both internal and external matters of the family of which the wife is the foundation. That is to say, they are interdependent although the husband has the responsibility for the whole family. It may also be mentioned that a woman is worth half a man in matters relating to ransom for a murder, inheritance, and the giving of evidence. The Qur'an grants to the husband "the right of severe correction". But the husband is required by tradition to treat his wife with kindness and moderation. The position of the wife, on the other hand, in conjugal life depends, as it does elsewhere, on her individual quality family life, to act regularly and consistently, thus to ensure that her opinions are listened to. Some wives exercise their authority over the members of the family, which is totally unjustified for the sake of the family's well-being. However, Muslim law has the provision to expose the wife to the public before any severe action is taken by husband. If the situation does not change, the husband is allowed to marry an additional wife whose presence can greatly modify the nature of the family life. The Hanafi rite, it should be stated here, acknowledged by modern jurists, eventually allows the divorce (talaq), "that is, the introduction into the marriage contract of clauses requiring the husband to repudiate his wife, and so to give her freedom, if certain circumstances should arise, if, for example, he marries another wife, if he absents himself for too long periods from the conjugal domicile, if he does not permit his wife to pay frequent visits to family or to stay with them, and so on"(12).

Eventually, the dogma allows the husband to be absent for a long time for purposes like pilgrimage and business. Interestingly, a pre-Islamic rule allowed the husband, when living away from home to marry a woman temporarily for enjoyment or to save him from loneliness, which is called "enjoyment"(mu'ta'), or temporary with the clear consent of the girl, of course. The Prophet Muhammad made it legal for his soldiers. However, Caliph 'Umar called it "sensual indulgence". At any rate, during the pre-Islamic time, it was accepted. In Mecca for the pilgrims, who resumed a kind of rite, the sexual relations which is forbidden during the period of their sanctity (ihram), no mu'ta' was allowed.

Modern society, save certain social classes, has maintained the ancient idea of the separation of husband and wife into two "clans". The wife is allowed to show her face only to men between whom and herself no marriage is allowed. Finally, the wearing of the veil or burqa is the external manifestation of this principle.

It may be pointed out here that the pre-Islamic Arabian marriage was annuled by the unilateral will of the husband, and by the spoken word of a formula of rejection, or by the return of the wife to the protection of her family. Muslim rule does not recognise this kind of marriage dissolution. A husband (muslim) can reject his wife at his own will or pleasure, she then gaining her liberty, and receiving the balance of the dowry which remained unpaid at the time of the contract. However, to make the divorce legal, he only needs to utter, at any time or place or occasion, by uttering the words expressing his repudiation (divorce). However, if he is a minor (<u>nabaleg</u>), his tutor or guardian intervenes.

According to the Qur'anic verses, the divorced wife should be kept under supervision. If she is found pregnant, the paternity or fatherhood of the child should be assigned to the husband, and the wife must receive proper maintenance until her confinement. The law, therefore, declared a waiting period ('<u>idda</u>) of three menstrual periods (<u>qura</u>'), during which the wife must be maintained by her husband and at the end of which, if not pregnant, the repudiation becomes final. To be sure, this waiting period was used to change slightly the effects of a quick divorce; so long as it has not ended, the husband can take his wife back without any condition or formality. But a second divorce or repudiation may be cancelled in the same way; the third is final. Notwithstanding the above-mentioned formula, the Qur'an says, "if the wife contracted marriage with a third party, and that was dissolved, she again became lawful (<u>halal</u>) for her first husband. This decision allows the use of a convenience "by which a third repudiation may be cancelled; an accommodating man agrees, for honourable payment, to contract an unconsummated marriage with the woman, repudiating her immediately, thus permitting the marriage"(13).

It should be stated here emphatically that divorce puts the husband under obligation to pay to the wife the total amount for her <u>mahar</u>. He will, naturally, be trying to subject her to a sort of treatment which will make her life painful and which will force her to buy his repudiation by cancelling her dowry, or under certain circumstances, even by payment of a compensation. Under these circumstances, with the admitted impotence of the husband, it is one of the cases in which the law permits the wife to have the right to go to the authority of the <u>qadi</u>, who can or may force the husband to repudiate or divorce her, and to pay her, her dowry.

In the light of the above discussion, it should be stated that in modern Muslim countries, moral habits and the development of the economic life, tend to create new rules which abandon the abuses of the law of divorce, such as the <u>jabar</u> and the marriage of young children. However, there is a common inclination towards European legislation on this subject. For example, in 1926, Turkey, a highly Westernised Muslim country, "adopted the Swiss Civil Code and abolished repudiation"(14).

By the way. the principal aim of the Qur'anic law in the case of marriage is to improve the position of the woman which was still very unjust and unfavourable compared with the pre-Islamic situation. "Thus, the marriage contract was made between the suitor and the guardian (father or the nearest male relative of the bride), the latter's consent was not regarded essential. But the <u>mahar</u> (bridal gift) was given to the bride herself, not to anyone else. "In marriage, the woman was under the unrestricted authority of her husband . . . Dissolution of the marriage rested entirely on the man's opinion; and even after his death, his relatives could enforce claims upon his widow"(15).

The regulations guiding marriage are the most important in principle and are laid down in some verses of the <u>sura</u> 4: (shortly after the battle of Uhud): 3." And if ye fear that ye will not deal fairly by the orphans, marry of the women, who seem good to you, two or three or four; and if ye fear that ye cannot do justice (to so many) then one (only) or (the captives) that your right hands possess. 4: And give unto the women, (whom ye marry) free gift of their marriage portions; but if they of their own accord remit unto you a part thereof, then ye are welcome to absorb it (in your wealth); and 22: "Marry not the women whom your fathers have married, except bygone; for this is shameful and abominable and an evil way. 23: "Forbidden to you are your mothers, your daughters, your sisters, your aunts paternal and maternal, the daughters of your brothers and sisters, your foster mothers and foster sisters, the mothers of your wives and your step-daughters who are in your care, born of your wives, with whom you have had intercourse—but if ye have not had intercourse with them, it is no sin for you—and the wives of your sons, who are your offspring, also that ye do not form a connection between two sisters, except bygones; Allah is forgiving and merciful". 24: "And all married women are forbidden unto you (except those captives) whom your right hands possess. It is a decree of Allah for you. Lawful unto you are all beyond those mentioned, so that ye seek them with your wealth in honest wed-lock, not debauchery. And those of whom ye <u>seek</u> content (by marrying them), give unto them their portions as a duty. And there is no sin for you in what ye do by mutual agreement after the duty (hath been done). Allah is ever knower, wise". 25: "And whoso is not able to afford to marry free, believing woman, let them marry from the believing maids, whom your right hand posseses. Allah knoweth best (concerning) your faith. Ye (proceed) one from another; so wed them by permission of their folk, and give unto them their portions in kindness, they being honest, not debouched nor of loose conduct. And if when they are honourably married, they commit lewdness, they shall incur the half of the punishment (prescribed) for free women (in that case)). This is for him among you who feareth to commit sin. But to have patience would be better for you. "Allah is Forgiving, Merciful". There is in <u>sura</u> 2. 221, the prohibition of marriage with infidels, male or female (1x. 10), in <u>sura</u> 33. 50, one exception in favour of the Prophet, and in <u>sura</u> 5.5: (of the Farewell Pilgrimage of the year 10) the permission of marriage with the women of the possessors of a sacred scripture (Jews and Christians). There are other verses of the Qur'an which emphasise the moral side of the marriage are sura 24. 3, 26, 32 and sura 30. 20.

Other important regulations concerning marriage are the number of wives allowed at one time to four even though sura 4.3 contains other alternatives. It should be clearly stated here that the cooperation of the "guardians", the dowry and the consent of the woman are considered as essential thus uncompromising, and competition with a rival whose case is still pending or unsettled is forbidden (16).

Finally, alongside of the normal form of the pre-Islamic Arab marriage which in spite of its looseness, aimed at the foundation of a household and the procreation of children, there was the practice of temporary marriage in which the couple lived together for a short period of time previously fixed. "Such temporary marriages were entered upon mainly by men who found themselves staying for a time abroad"(17). It is by no means certain that these are referred to in sura 4. 24, although the Muslim name for this marriage muta' (temporary marriage of sexual pleasure) is based on the wording of the verse; it is, however, certain from the hadith that the Prophet really permitted muta' to his followers especially on the longer campaigns. But the Caliph 'Umar strictly abandoned muta' and considered it as fornication (zina') some traditions say that the Prophet himself prohibited it.

Regarding talaq (divorce), the Doctrine has allowed that, if the husband utters such a formula as "Thou are repudiated three times" the repudiation is final. The repudiation compels the husband to pay to the wife the whole amount of her dowry. In retaliation, he may subject his wife to unbearable treatment which will force her to buy his repudiation by abandoning her dowry, or even by paying an indemnity. Under these circumstances, the law allows the wife to appeal to the authority of the <u>qadi</u>, who may force the husband to divorce her and to pay her, her dowry. The situations described here have been regulated by the jurists (<u>fuqaha</u>) of the four schools of jurisprudence (18).

In passing, it should be mentioned that the Qur'an has allowed polygamy (polygyny) which was usual among the Bedouin, but it has limited to four the number of wives a man may have at one time. It has also maintained the "serial polygamy of the repudiation, not to mention concubinage and prostitution" (19). Nevertheless, the custom maintained that it is better to have only one wife, monogamy; in fact, it was forced upon those who live a settled life, especially upon city dwellers with their present day economic condition and customs.

At this stage, let us say a few words about the family of the Prophet Muhammad: To begin with, there has been a lot of misunderstanding and misjudgement regarding his marriages. Thus an author says, "There has been much loose talk about the exception made by the Qur'an in favour of Muhammad in the matter of the number of his wives". "But it should be recognized that the history of the wives and children of the Prophet is a confused succession of improbabilities", continues the learned author, "in which it is not possible to discern the truth. It can at least be remembered that it was in accordance with custom that the Chief should have more wives than the other members of the clan. Moreover, Muhammad's marriages were for the most part political alliances: Hafsa is the daughter of 'Umar, Umm Habiba, the child of Abu Sufyan, 'A'sha is the daughter of Abu Bakr; Safiya, the Jewess, is the daughter of a conquered chief, and therefore was assigned as legal booty to the victor"(20). Moreover, some of his wives were actually volunteer maids as they wanted to be, but the Prophet, who had no custom of maintaining maids at his home, he allowed them to stay at his home only as his wives. Interestingly, the Egyptian girl, Hafsa, who walked all the way from her home to Madina to serve the Prophet, could stay at his home only as his wife rather than as his maid. At one time, he had as many as 13 wives, but had only one son, Qasim. This fact tells us clearly that the Prophet had really no family life, as we have. How could he? Within a period of ten years, he had to fight sixty-eight battles (gozwa and sarya): he was the commander-in-chief of the sixteen gozwa, and the fifty-two saryas were commanded by his assistants. That is to say, he had hardly any time for a full-time family life, an obligation for a married man.

The next important issue is the farjand (children). The children born of the husband's wives form his family, only if they were born six months after the "consummation of the marriage, or up to four years after its dissolution". The family receives and gives equal rights to the child born of a concubine. The husband may dispute, by the special channel of the oath of "malediction" (li'an), the paternity of his wife's child.

In passing, it may be mentioned that the pre-Islamic Arab family was completed by the inclusion of the slaves. The Qur'an maintained or retained slavery while recommending that they should be well treated and set free.

In Islam there are laws concerning slave marriage. Briefly, a slave is married to a slave. This is the simple rule. A slave's dowry is half of a free woman's; a female slave may marry either a free man or slave; their children are slaves of the woman's master. However, a master may not marry a slave unless he first frees her; otherwise she is a concubine, and her status is recognized by Muslim law. The slave who gives a child to her master is called "child's mother' (umm walad); the child is free and is treated like a legitimate child, and the mother gains her freedom with the death of her husband (21).

Muslim Social Life

To begin with, it is well-known that the life of the Muslims differs so much from one period to another, and from one country to another, has always been brightened by a number of ceremonies and practices which are, more or less, common to all Muslims.

The birth of son for a Muslim family is a joyful event as opposed to the birth of a daughter. It should be mentioned here that some pre-Islamic Arabs often buried their daughter alive following their birth. Prophetic tradition sanctioned the ancient usage by which a birth was celebrated by the shaving of the head and offering of a living sacrifice"(22). On the seventh day following the birth, two sheep or goats were sacrificed and their meat offered to the poor Muslims. Simultaneously, alms were given in the form of a sum of silver equal to the weight of the infant's hair which was "ceremoniously removed". This ceremony is called 'aqiqa. Following the child's birth, which is considered a happy occasion, one person pronounces adhan (call to prayer) in to the child's right ear, and those of the iqama into his left ear, so as to accustom him to the Muslim confession of faith"(23). It is a widespread practice among the Muslim families that the name-giving ceremony ('aqiqa) is held on the 7th day of the child's birth. It may be pointed out that names usually are in Arabic; however, sometimes there are names in Turkish, Persian or even Berber names still in vogue. There are also some saints' names, whose influence extends over a vast area: "Shu'ayb and Bu Medien are current in Oramia, around the sanctuary of Saidi Bu Medien at El-Eubbad near Tlemcen; Jilali and Jalul are as common as the qubbas of Sidi 'Abbd al-Qadir al-Jilani"(24). However, the real Muslim names are those of the Prophets: Muhammad, Ahmad (also in Turkish Mehmet and Mahammed, Mustafa or Mostfa; of the members of the Prophet's family: Hasan. Husayn, 'Ali, and also of the well-known personalities of Muslim tradition: Musa, Sulayman,

Ibrahim, Isma'il, Ishaq, Daud, 'Abdullah ("Servant of Allah"), Abu Bakr, 'Umar, 'Uthman; sometimes God's names are replaced by one of His ninety-nine appellations (sifat) such as al-Qadir, al-Rahman, al-Rahim, al-Salam, al-Razzaq, al-Hamid, al-'Aziz, al-Haqq, etc.

It should be stated here that the name of a child is completed by adding that of the father; e. g. Ahmad ibn Muhammad, and by other elements as well: first by a kunya which reproduces the name of the first son after the word "father of: Abu al-Qasim (Muhammad), Abu Uthman, Abu Tashfin, etc. It may also be a nickname (laqab): e. g. Nur al-Din (light of the faith), Bu Baghla (the mule man), Bu Amama (the man with the turban), al-Aswad (the black), etc.; or else an attribute (nisba): al-Sabbagh (the dyer), al-Baghdadi (the man of Baghdad), al-Madani); etc. Daughters usually receive the names of the woman of the family of the Prophet, Khdija, Fatima, 'A'isha, Zaynab, etc.; there may be names of attributes or of flowers, such as Mabruka (blessed), Mahbuba (beloved), Sharifa (noble), Maya, Zena, etc.

According to the tradition, the baby belongs completely to mother; if she is able to do so, she feeds the baby for two years. The mother's primary anxiety is to protect the baby from the evil eye by all means.

For a male child, circumcisionis a rite which is strictly followed all over the Muslim World, even though it is not prescribed by the Qur'an. It is performed either on the seventh day, or on the fortieth, or in the seventh year, "that is at the beginning of the second period of life"(25). The accompanying ceremonies are celebrated according to the status and capacity of the family. It may be mentioned that they sometimes show a similarity with marriage: "both are transitionary rites". It is a widespread custom to give presents to the boy on this occasion, as on the occasion before his marriage.

The young boys are brought up by their mothers until they reach the age of seven years. At that age, he starts his life as a man, either by helping his father with his work, whatever he can do, or by beginning the study of the Qurr'an at school (<u>maktab</u>). At school, the boy learns how to read and write down the Qur'an by a mechanical effort. On a piece of paper or a board, he tries to write words from the Qur'an, and also learns by heart, but without any attempt yet to understand the meaning which is beyond his capacity as a child, but he acquires the rhythm and chanting of it. When the boy has learned a part of the Qur'an (<u>juz</u>), his family gives a feast for his master (<u>ustad</u>) and friends. A more significant ceremony is celebrated when the boy has finished the memorising of the Qur'an (<u>hifz</u>) and became a <u>hafiz-i-Qur'an</u> (the Qur'an memoriser). We are told that "Ibn Jubayr reproduces for our benefit the <u>khutba</u> that the young Hafiz preached on the evenings of Ramadan in the 13th century in the mosque of Madina, and which were followed by a banquet given by the father"(26).

In addition to the Qur'an learning, some lessons of grammar and arithmetic were added to the programme. Ibn Khaldun protested the exclusive teaching of the Qur'an excluding other subjects; then included other subjects, the ones mentioned above. Commenting on the above-mentioned system of education, G-Demombynes says, "with many children a natural gift for understanding the mechanics of the language, it could almost be called a philological sense, enabled them to achieve a satisfactory education in spite of the very rudimentary nature of its beginnings"(27).

Having achieved the above-mentioned knowledge, the young boy enters into a wider field of education which includes all branches of Islamic education such as the <u>tafsir, hadith, fiqh, usul al-fiqh,</u> grammar, lexicography, rhetoric, literature.

Memorising the lessons was the general practice of those days. The teaching or schooling took place usually in the teacher's home, in the absence of a public building for schooling. But often teaching took place in the nearby mosque, if it was possible. The teacher was seated in the middle of the circle either on the floor or, if possible, on a platform (kursi). A passage from a classical book or from the Qur'an was read and the teacher explained it; a few notes were taken, though, but it was primarily memorising to retain the lessons. As for the curriculum, it was fixed by the teacher as he considered useful: "assiduous and capable listeners received his authority to repeat his lessons in another city, a licenciadocendi (ijaza) (28). Through this process, some of the important books of well-known authors were sent around, and their teachings went around all over the Muslim world.

This organisation, well-known to the Western Middle Ages, had, in the East, been spread and given a wider opportunity. For instance, 'Abbasid caliphs opened dar al-hadith (Houses of the Tradition): Al-Ma'mun opened a "House of Knowledge"(dar al-'ilm), which the Egyptian Fatimids eventually copied in Egypt, and of which the Mosque of Al-Azhar is an exalted institution. By the way, this University of Cairo has been copied in the Muslim West, in the Zaituna of Tunis and the Qarawuyan of Fez.

Following the above-mentioned examples, during the 11th and 12th centuries some rulers like Nizam al-Mulk, Nur al-Din Zangi, and others like them, established schools of cannon law (fiqh), which were actually types of "seminaries" for the study of the practice of religion. These madrasas gave rise to the influential corporation of the fuqaha' (jurists), an organised doctrine and a coherent beginning. (29).

At this stage, let us say a few words about the girls: It is well-known that a girl in a family is by nature a helping hand—to her mother, to begin with. As she grows up, before her marriage, she is the constant helper of her mother until the culture of "maid" became popular among the well-to-do families. The girls also learn the trade of their families whatever it is. In the classical time of Muslim society, cultured women were found in the upper classes of the 'Abbasid Empire. But it was slaves as well as free women who were skilled in the arts, music, songs and dances; they were often given an extensive education in this field. The "Book of Songs" (Aghani) gives examples of such, and "Tawaddud the Learned Woman" is one of the tales of the Arabian Nights"(30).

In the modern Islamic world, there is a sharp difference between the traditional Muslim family and the modern one. In the field of education, in particular, there are Qur'anic schools and also madrasas for purely Islamic education. That gives the Muslim children a wide range of opportunity to obtain knowledge about both religion and family matters; there are schools in the mosques as well. On the continent of Africa, there are French schools open to all religious-social classes of students including Muslims. In other Middle-Eastern Muslim countries like Egypt, Syria, Turkey, Iraq, Lebanon and others, there are schools from primary to secondary levels, as well as colleges and universities to offer all kinds of education of modern times. The University of Cairo is a world-famous seat of knowledge whence the word of chair, thus chairman, became famous all over the world. On the sub-continent of Bangladesh, India and Pakistan, there are schools and universities, especially those of 'Aligarh and Haiderabad are world famous as the number one seats for seeking knowledge. In Bangladesh, there exists one of the well-known madrasahs named: Madrasah 'Alia, originally existed in Calcutta before the partition of the sub-continent of India in 1947. These and other universities are supported by a well-organised system of elementary and secondary systems of education. In today's world, Islamic education is taught in some Western Universities like the Institute of Islamic Studies, McGill University, Montreal, Quebec, Canada, established in 1952, the first of this kind in the Western World.

It may be pointed out here that the worldwide woman's movement is helping women to have a share in the development of education. During the last century, some Muslim girls had been able to achieve some academic excellence having education in Christian schools, "where they had not on the same benches with Catholic and Protestant girls"(31). It is also well-known that during the last few years, national schools for girls have been opened in many countries especially in Turkey and in the Middle Eastern countries where secondary education, in particular, has been making unabated progress; and all over the Muslim world, higher education is now available to Muslim students.

A young man gets married around twenty years of age. The nature of his married life varies almost endlessly. There is the father-oriented (patriarchal) family, where all the members of the family remain united as long as the head of the family (father or grandfather) remains alive. Then the couple lives a completely modern couple's life mostly in the cities. As well, housing conditions reflect the diversity in the family life. There are modern, ultra-modern mansions like banglos, flats or condomoniums, with an electrical power system, "the sprawling palace sheltering several branches of one family, the classical Mediterranean dwelling, a tent, a hut, a troglodyte cover"(32).

When we discuss the story of the palaces of the Caliphs, Sultans and other great Muslims like the ministers, we find information in the pages of history books. Thus one writer says, "At the two ends of

Islam, both of space and time, there remain the castles of the Umayyads of Syria and the palace of the Nasrids, the Alhambra (al-hambra', the red) at Granada. The fragments which still stand at Mshatta, at Qusayr 'Amra, at Qusayr al-Hair, etc., witness to the past existence of buildings so perfect and so grandiose, that archaeologists have difficulty in believing that they are not of Sasanid origin"(33). The heirs of the kings, the 'Abbasids, have left the buildings or edifices which they built of materials more charming, vast and tall pavilion in which they had the space for their official reception, ('iwan), and the traditional architecture of the Iranian model. The residences (palaces) of the Caliph, consisted of many facilities such as isolated pavilions in gardens; there were also lakes surrounded by trees, "and brooks fringed with banks that were beds of flowers, belveders on the Tigris, frail edifices whose splendor lay in their decorations in the shape of mosaics, pierced stucco, frescoes, emphasised by the brilliance of the hangings that adorned the walls, and the carpets underfoot; all short-lived things"(34). There were some princes who had their own palaces or pavilions built according to their own choice and interest or pleasure. For the summer time, there were provisions to keep the palace cool with melting snow.

In Arabia (Hijaz, Yemen), in particular, there were homes of several floors: there were citadels for defence; there were underground rooms for shelter from extreme heat. Notwithstanding the above information, the Mediterranean house on a single floor is still the ideal dwelling. There were homes with water pool. Everywhere niches in the walls form recesses, are made into cupboards, or fitted with shelves. In one corner, a stairway leads up to the terraces on which are often found an upper room; the terrace is the women's area and a place of shelter on summer nights. Externally, the walls are plain, with, of course, some windows. The interior is completely screened from the eyes of the people, and defended from the intruders. As for the furniture, there were only a few like chairs and stools; some mattresses and carpets on the floor; articles of everyday use, like bowls, earthenware vases that are used at home.

As for the men of the family, they are most of the time out of the home gathering essentials for the family like food and all related things for which they go to shops and markets, pass the time socialising with friends often in <u>suq</u> (tavern). "Much card playing is indulged in today around the shores of the Mediterranean; in early days, and in spite of the prohibition of the <u>hadith</u> that supplemented the Qur'an, games of chances of many kinds were played on a draught board; a few authorities tolerate chess because of the absence of the element of chance and the royal tradition that India and Persia have given it"(35). Also there were horse racing and betting, pigeon racing and cock-fighting. Since there were no other outdoor games of pleasure like the ones that are in to day's world, for instance, all kinds of outdoor entertainments, like musical programmes, dancing and singing; they enjoyed whatever they had in those days, as mentioned above.

Physical sports like wrestling were very popular. The game of soccer was a very popular and outdoor enjoyable sport. One of the traditional childish battles was the play with a sling. During the feasts, there were games of skill at the 'Umra in Mecca as well as at marriage, circumcisions and other family events like birthday celebrations.

It is reported that old texts recommended the learning of the art of swimming, interesting in a country like Arabia, where there are not even ponds or pools, save irrigation tanks. The practice of hot bath, a Syrian custom, adopted in Arabia, which, in addition to its sanitary merits, "fell in admirably with the obligation of legal purity (<u>tahara</u>) imposed on Muslims"(36). The layout of the baths varies nominally only in details, and the actual needs they provide make sure their practical similarity with the Roman baths. The owner (mu'allim) is present to offer coffee; in the next room, there are facilities for warming up and undressing and resting, especially in winter time. There are other facilities such as sweating room, then hot and cold rooms, etc. The customer is given a massage and bathed by a bath-attendant in the harara (small room). Interestingly, the ladies of a family take great pleasure in hiring a bath for the afternoon and there making amusement with their female relatives and friends. Well-to-do families used to keep a hammam in their house.

The next great occasion is the celebration of feast days in Muslim life. The two important feasts are the anniversary of the sacrifice of the hajj (pilgrimage), and that of the breaking of the Ramadan fast. The "great feast ('id al-adha, 'id al-qurban, al-'id al-kabir, in Turkish, buyuk bayram) commemorates the 10th of dhul hajja, the day of the nahr which, at Mina, marks the end of the ceremonies of the pilgrimage; each family offers up, in accordance with the ritual, a camel or a sheep, which then becomes the basis of a banquet in which the poor have their share"(37).Then comes the 'id a-fitr, celebration of the first day of the month of shawwal following the end of the month of Ramadan. For the Muslims, rich and poor, it is a day of joy, to put on new clothes to perform the 'id prayer, held in mosques or the large congregation held in outdoor places (musalla); to exchange hugs and kisses, and gifts and congratulations, according to the hadith advice.

The feast of the birth of the Prophet Muhammad (milad) is celebrated all over the Muslim world on the 10the of rabi' 1. 'Ashura' is raised to the level of a feast, and has gained "carnivalesque" or carnivorous rites, particularly on the African continent (Berber region). (On the same day, the Shi'ites celebrate the anniversary of the death of Husayn at Karbala [672] by the performance of a Passion play (ta'zia) and with processions, in the course of which fanatical worshipers beat their bodies and faces until the blood flows. (38). All over the Muslim world, there are additional celebrations apart from the official ones: rites, sometimes more enthusiastically observed than they themselves are, associated with the anniversaries of the saints (musem) and others which are survivals of ancient religion and seasonal rites. The qubbas or majar of the saints have always been the object of frequent visits by the women, who carry there their offerings.

It should be noted here that the feasts provide an opportunity for showing the resources of the restaurant that is governed by local custom. We are told that "The hadith attempted to enforce the observance of Muslim rules by noting the likes and dislikes of the Prophet; at least it gave the force of law to the customs that fix the standard of conduct during meals"(39).The rich people began to show a liking of Western crockery. For sure, cooking in the Muslim world resists outside influence more vigorously than is the case with dress. If the clothing of the Bedouin and the peasant (fallah) preserves its ancient appearance, shirt or qamis, drawers (sirwall), a cloak covering the shoulders and body (rida'); if legal officials, Qadis, muftis, imams, fuqaha, still wear the classical garments, over which are thrown white draperies; if a part of the city population still remains faithful to the loose trousers, waistcoats, jackets, and embroidered caftans, delicately coloured cloth below a gray mantle; if manual workers still working, particularly in the maghrib (West), abandoned those traditional "overcoats," "the barnus and the jallaba, the generality, whether rich or poor, are more and more adopting European costume, which is doubtless more practical, less costly, and less durable; and most unfortunate from the point of view of the beauty of the silhouettes and colours of a Muslim street"(40).

Most city-ladies do wear traditional clothing as long as they are at home. Outside the home, they wear a dress which covers their body fully. Some orthodox ladies wear <u>salwar</u> and <u>qamis</u> and some even <u>burqa</u>. City-dwelling women easily got accustomed to Western fashions in all respects. "European fashions, with the suppression or diminution of the veil, are invading the Orient and destroying its originality"(41).

Ornaments are used according to the occasion and place, diverse variety of form: ear-rings, diadems, necklaces, pendents, bracelets and rings are used. The materials used differ greatly: for the rich, gold silver, precious stones, pearls; copper tinsel and iron for the poor. "During the feasts and at a marriage, a great show of jewels is demanded; from early days, the hiring of jewelry was a very profitable business"(42).

Fashions in hairdressing and in headdresses have differed widely. The Bedouins still keep their hair long, probably a kind of head-covering against the desert-heating; they wear a light turban. In the cities, the turban became more complicated after the 9th century when its size increased to the laughable size. "The fashion of the enormous turban spread at the same time as that of the shaven head and felt cap or <u>shasliya</u>. But, at the end of the 12th century, for example, the people of Baghdad still affected the pendant locks which they piously offer as a sacrifice to the scissors of some persuasive maker of sermons"(43). For beauty, the beard, often the hair as well, was died with <u>henna/mehendi</u>. It is well-known that the reddish hair colour of <u>henna</u> was recommended following the Prophet's practice. At the present time, the adoption of Western fashion is driving to a widespread use of the razor.

During the present age, there is no more ancient culture of tribal fighting using all kinds of traditional weapons like the sabre, the javelin and the lances and the shield and coat of mail for protection. By the way, 18th century Arabia had archers, and archery has survived to the present day as a traditional sport. During the Crusades, there were development of mechanical weapons and Greek fire. The "crossbow" became one of the arms of the Muslim forces, then firearms.

There was a popular belief for hundred of years that illness is the result of the tricks of <u>satan,</u> of the jinns, of wizards and witches; then the sick person must get treatment by the use of magical counter-measures. But medical science, invented and spread by the Greeks, had spread all over the Orient before the Muslim conquests; Abbasid <u>khalifas</u> (caliphs) had Greek physicians trained in the school at Gundishapure. Then during the days of their political powers, Muslims collected and added to the observation of Greek medicine and also philosophy; it was they who first introduced them to Europe (44). The Muslim world of the 9th century (Baghdad, 894), had its first hospitals, called first <u>bimaristan</u> ("place of the sick"). In the tenth century, there were hospitals established in the cities by the order of the Caliphs who provided money to pay the doctors and pharmacists and maintenance of the sick people by creating <u>hubus</u>; by the 12th century there were established <u>mustashfa</u> (healing place) (45). In the tenth century, an Iranian physician attempted to regulate the profession of medicine.

Death is also associated with rites, of which some are prescribed by the <u>shari'ah</u> and others are a continuation from the ancient customs; some are not in agreement with the <u>shari'ah</u>. When a sick person is about to die, his family turns his head towards the <u>qibla,</u> and recites the <u>shahada</u> in his name. The family's mourning begins instantly. Nevertheless, the body is ready for washing, in accordance with the customs of Islam—with requirements of the greater ablution (<u>ghusl</u>) by two persons of the same sex as the dead person. This is done only by persons who have the knowledge of rites; the <u>ghossal</u> or <u>mughassil</u> performs for him an act of piety for which they will be rewarded on the Day of Judgement. It is an innovation (bid'a) to the washers deceased's clothing. "The orifices of the body are closed with plugs of perfumed cotton wool, and the body itself is wrapped in one or two pieces of seamless clothes; certain traditions tell that it is in this garment that the dead person will appear before God"(46). In passing, it may be mentioned here that the pilgrims carry their grave clothes with them to Mecca, there to dip them in the water of Zamzam.

The time of burial takes place as soon as possible to avoid non-Islamic practices of keeping the dead body for a period of mourning. In some families, ancient and modern women maintain the traditional lamentations (walwal), during which they beat themselves on the face and breast, etc. People of the neighbourhood assemble to take part in the funeral service, expressing their words of praise for the deceased and sympathy for the dead person's family. "Such praise takes the form of the chanting of short, rhythmical phrases of rhymed prose or verse, accompanied by the beating of a tambourine"(47).

It should also be mentioned here that the woman who is in charge of the duty of making the funeral oration (nadiba) is sometimes qualified with the poetical talent: thus, the pious completion of the rite has come to be entrusted to professionals. "Both the lamentations and the praising of the dead, of which pre-Islamic Arabia provides, in the poems of Al-Khausa', brilliant examples, condemned by certain apparently genuine hadith of the Prophet"(48).

The body is carried to the graveyard on the "trestle" on which it was washed, covered only by a white cloth. Continuously changing relays of four men carrying it on their shoulders—this is a pious work which will be rewarded in the next life. At the head of the procession, walk the religious persons ('ulama, ikhwan of brotherhood, who chant the <u>kalima</u> and <u>du'a</u> (Muslim confession of faith and fragments of religious poems). Eventually, the dead body is brought to a mosque where a larger than usual congregation performs the "prayer of dead" (<u>salat al-janaza</u>). In all other places where the dead are excluded from the mosque, this prayer is performed either in the cemetery or in a special place called <u>bayt al-janaza</u>, attached to the mosque and located behind the <u>mihrab</u>. The tomb is designed like a chamber to place the body to lie on the right side, with the head pointing to Mecca, untied the knots of the cloth.

Some <u>hadith</u> disapprove of the building of the rounded mounds which cover the tombs, and disapprove more vigorously of the monuments that "crown" them. The practice of constructing buildings on them began to become popular during the 10th century C. E. The tombs of the Mamluk Sultans in Cairo are the best examples of the many "funerary mosques that are to found throughout the Orient"(49).

It is a common belief among people, not all certainly, for sure, that their dead survived in another life in which their worldly needs would continue, "and they have believed that the articles that had been in their households had been soiled by some evil spell" (50). Sometimes it is difficult to know exactly which of those two ideas survives in the practice of destroying all that had belonged to the dead person. It is reported that in Baghdad, for instance, during the 10th century C. E., the above-mentioned practice was used even in the boat which had taken the body to the river. "It is the first idea, complicated by that of the efficacy of the prayer for the dead, which preserves among Muslims certain customs that are also well-known to other peoples; the funeral banquet repeated on various days, visit paid to the cemetery accompanied by the performance of certain rites, animal sacrifices, alms giving, etc."(51).

The cemetery is frequently visited by the Muslim community, including the women. Some graveyards are located at convenient locations for easy access for the visitors. There are some graveyards which are lighted for night visitors to pray. "Death is accepted with resignation, and the living who, apart from the compulsory rites, do not pretend to a grief that the joy of living quickly dissipates, frequent without sorrow the places of the dead, to whom they bring the tender tribute of memory"(52).

There was another demeaning or shameful practice in Muslim society, viz., slavery: "although never of a particularly odious character in the Muslim world, it was the cause of the evil reputation it acquired in matters of sexual morality". "The presence of young slaves and eunuchs in rich families encouraged sodomy, which was, and still is, one of the vices of Muslim society; it was so common among all classes that the Doctrine hesitated to condemn it"(53).

On the other hand, female slavery, by providing the owner with concubines, emphasised the disorders that polygamy could not fail to cause within the family, and yet free the Muslim society of prostitution. During the tenth century of the Christian Era, the moral desirability of monogamy was being preached, but it was just then that indecency in literature was widely prevalent.

Through a gradual process of reformation, the Qur'an finally forbade the consumption of alcohol (cf. Q. 2. 219; 4. 43; 5. 90f.).

The pre-Islamic Arabians had been inspired by a strong feeling of muruwwa, ("virility"), that is, of the qualities that make a man fit to defend his dignity or honour ('ird) and of his tribe. However, Islam put in place for 'ird the din (faith), and welcomed the Muslims "to do good and forbid evil", that is, to follow the divine commands and stay away from, and to prevent others from doing, what Allah forbids. In a nutshell, in Islam morality and piety become one and the same thing. Undoubtedly, the law insists on the importance of the intention (<u>niya</u>) which leads the Muslims to act "for the face of God"; but it was Sufism that appreciated to the full the driving force of love, and declared that love was the essential ingredient of merit in human action"(54). However, the dogma or teaching, on the other hand, has taken the secular and modern point of view, that of the public well-being, the <u>maslaha</u>, a sort of solidarity.

The maintenance of the family relationship is another of the vital foundations of the Muslim <u>Umma</u> (community). Although with the rise of Islam, many young people left their families in response to the call of the Prophet; to be sure, the Prophet never forced anyone to do so, for Islam does not allow compulsion in converting people to it. The respect in which the children hold their parents is as much a fact of Muslim life as it is a provision of the law. The Qur'an and the Tradition (<u>hadith</u>) have given attention to the civilized behavior of women (cf. Q. 24.31). The Qur'an ordains justice and honesty towards all men, respect for weights and measures, fidelity to engagement and oaths, the delivery to the real owner of that which is received in trust, etc. Some historians have talked about "Islamic socialism". Undoubtedly, the Prophet tried to improve the conditions of the weak and the prisoners, of slaves and wives, and of the widows and the orphans of the Muslim warfare. Notwithstanding the existence of wealthy and authoritative individuals in a Muslim society, the feeling of equality and brotherhood of all Muslims is still alive. The legal and moral obligation of alms-giving is not an attack on the rich; "it is a means of purification, a guaranty against a compensatory reaction in the life to come, in which excessive enjoyment of the things of this life will find its retribution"(55). Indirectly, it helps people to get rid of what is called the nasty vice of vices, pride (<u>takabbur</u>), the vice which stopped Iblis from bowing down before Adam as Allah commanded him, and by which he was lost.

Finally, according to Islamic ethics and morality, "The believer must avoid contempt and arrogance and show, in all his actions, and even in his gait, humility sustained by gravity." "Islam condemns greed and avarice, but also the prodigality which was once a point of honour for the Arab"(56).

To conclude, Islamic tradition insists on some decorum and courtesy in Muslims' day-to-day life, for it has some connection with morality. Islamic morality has been highly practised and encouraged by Sufism and philosophers in order to rise to a higher stage of humanity along with religious practice, supplemented by some virtues.

CHAPTER 5 : References

1. Gaudefray-Demombynes, Maurice, <u>Muslim Institutiones:
   Dominion, Community, Ideas, Dogma, Law, Cult, Caliphate
   Family, Property, Justice Social Life. Economic Life Intellectual
   Life. Modern Life,</u> (translated from the French by John P.
   Macgregor: Les Institutions Musulmans), George Allen &
   Unwin LTD, London, 1956, P. 127.
2. <u>Ibid.</u>, p.128; cf. Schacht, J., "Nikah", <u>Shorter Encyclopaedia of
   Islam (SEI),</u> pp. 447-449.
3. <u>Ibid.</u>; also cf. Spies, O., "Mohr" original "purchase money",
   <u>SEI</u>, pp. 314f.
4. <u>Ibid.</u>, P. 129; also cf. Schacht, <u>op. cit.</u>, p. 447.
5. <u>Ibid.</u>, also cf. Schacht, <u>op. cit.</u>, p. 447.
6. G-Demombynes, <u>op.cit.</u>, p. 129; also cf. Schacht, <u>op. cit.</u>, p.448.
7. <u>Ibid.</u>, p. 130.
8. <u>Ibid.</u> For more information about different types of marriage, cf.
   <u>ibid.</u>, pp. 130f.
9. <u>Ibid.</u>, p. 131.
10. <u>Ibid.</u>, p.132.
11. <u>Ibid.</u>
12. <u>Ibid.</u>
13. <u>Ibid.</u>, p. 134; also cf. Schacht, <u>op. Cit.</u>, p. 447. The differences
    in this matter among the four Schools of Jurisprudence are
    discussed thoroughly in many sources, thus cf. G-demombynes,
    <u>op. cit.</u>, p. 135.
14. G-Demombynes, <u>op. cit.</u>, p. 135.
15. Schacht, <u>op. cit.</u>, p.447.

16. For controversy among the Schools of Jurisprudence concerning the rules and practices relating to marriage, cf. SEI,op. cit., pp. 447f.
17. Ibid., p. 449.
18. For details on this subject, cf. G-Demombynes, op. cit., pp. 135f.
19. Ibid,. p. 136.
20. Ibid.
21. Cf. ibid., 137. For more information on slave marriage which is no longer practised in Islamic tradition, cf. ibid., pp. 137f.
22. G-Demombynes, op. cit., p. 159.
23. Ibid.
24. Ibid., p. 160.
25. Ibid., p. 161.
26. Ibid. op. cit., p. 162.
27. Ibid.
28. For more information about the rise and systematically organised Schools of Jurisprudence—Sunni and Shi'a, and Sufism, cf. ibid., pp. 163f.
29. Ibid., p. 164; also cf. J. Schacht, "Nikah", SEI, pp. 447ff.
30. G-Demombynes, op. cit., p. 165.
31. Ibid.
32. Ibid.
33. Ibid.
34. Ibid,. p. 166.
35. Ibid., p. 167.
36. Ibid., p. i68.
37. For more information about Shi'te rites, cf. ibid., p. 168.
38. G-Demombynes, op. Cit., p. 169.
39. Ibid.
40. Ibid.
41. Ibid.
42. Ibid., p.170.

43. Cf. <u>ibid</u>., p. 170.
44. Cf. <u>ibid</u>.
45. <u>Ibid</u>., p. 171.
46. <u>Ibid</u>.
47. <u>Ibid</u>.
48. <u>Ibid</u>., p. 172; for more information on this subject, cf. <u>Ibid</u>., pp. 172f.
49. <u>Ibid</u>., p. 173.
50. <u>Ibid</u>.
51. <u>Ibid</u>.
52. <u>Ibid</u>., p. 174.
53. <u>Ibid</u>. p. 175.
54. <u>Ibid</u>.
55. <u>Ibid</u>.

CHAPTER 6

<u>Islamic mysticism (Sufism)</u>

The word "<u>Sufi</u>" is derived either from "<u>Safa</u>" (pure) or "<u>saff</u>" (row) or "<u>suf</u>" (wool). As a matter of fact, the word is a derivative of all the above-mentioned roots to mean that <u>sufi</u> is a saintly person whose heart is believed to be pure, and who, as a sign of austerity, wears a woolen garment and who will stand in the first <u>saff</u> (row) on the day of judgement (1). However, there is another more detailed description of <u>Sufism</u> in the light of what the Prophet Muhammad was and the religion Islam, is: "True Sufism is a fusion of both physical and spiritual aspects of life. It is a hope against depression, a strength against spiritual weakness, a light against darkness, a race against sluggishness. Thus Sufism is the most noble way of Islamic dynamic life. The life of the Prophet Muhammad is the best example of this dynamic life: a man, a husband, a father, a Prophet and Preacher, a law-maker and reformer, a statesman, a soldier and commander-in-chief, and a great <u>sufi</u> who established the way, popularly known as the <u>tariqah'-I muhammadiyaah</u> (Muhammad's way of life). The practice of Sufism developed, however, not in the renunciation of the outer life but in bringing into its fold every aspect—a consciousness of God, a ceaseless vigil on purity of motive and inner integrity"(2). Mysticism is a global phenomenon of personal experience surpassing all religious or national identity. Hence, Evelyn Underhill says: "Though mystical theologies of the East and the West differ widely—though the ideas of life which they hold out to the soul differ too—yet in the experience of the soul this conflict is seen to be transcended; when the love of God is reached divergencies become impossible, for the soul has passed beyond the sphere of the manifold and is immersed in the One Reality"(3).

Hence, mystics of all religions and cultures are basically the same in their spiritual quest. Therefore, no one can find wide difference between a Muslim sufi (mystic), Hindu mystic or the Christian mystic at their last stage of spiritual journey. In this connection, A. J. Arberry says, "It has become a platitude to observe that mysticism is essentially one and the same, whatever may be the religion professed by the individual mystic: a constant and unvarying phenomenon of the universal yearning of the human spirit for personal communion with God"(4).

The above discussion has given a good understanding of the fact that mysticism is basically a global fact with the same aims and objectives. Thus, the mystics' way has always been the basic cause for their conflict with the orthodox version of all religions, and encouraged them to follow their natural policy of exchanging religious ideas with other religions.

It should be mentioned emphatically that fundamentally Sufism (tasawwuf) is rooted in the Qur'an (5). Prophet Muhammad's prophetic consciousness was founded upon definite and powerful mystic experiences, described in the Qur'an (17. 1; 53. 1-18; 81. 19-25). These verses support the truth of the Prophet's mission (e. g. 53. 11 f.; 81. 22f.). By the way, these verses had been revealed during the Meccan period. But during the Madinine period, following the rise of the Muslim community (ummah) and everything related to it, the sole mystical experiences were replaced by practical actions. Therefore, mysticism was materialised in the active or busy life of the Prophet Muhammad.

Among the first companions of the Prophet, there arose from the Prophet's teaching and his life-style, a sense of responsibility before the justice of Allah—fear of death—in the context of moral responsibilities as busy religious-social beings. "Among the Companions, there were some with whom this sense deepened into a special degree of inwardness of action, or the interiorization and introspection of the moral motive. This is exemplified by men like Abu Dharr al-ghefari, who formed the nucleus of Madinese piety after the Prophet. This became the foundation-stone of Muslim asceticism that developed rapidly during the later 1st./7th century and the 2nd./8th centuries"(6). It is also known that there was a group of twelve pious companions of the Prophet who abandoned the worldly life and attached themselves to the Prophet's Mosque (masjid-i-nabawi) at Madina, and were well known as the ahl as-suffa (people of the raised platform of the mosque)—those were the first known ascetics of Islamic Brotherhood. Later, beginning from the Umayyad period of Muslim government, which witnessed the unprecedented luxury of a Muslim Empire, the rise of the kharejites, provided opportunity to pietisim and to asceticism. For good, one of the most famous persons of this ethical piety was well-known Hasan al-Basrri (d. 110/728) "who not only won the recognition of his contemporaries but also exerted after his death one of the most powerful influences in the whole of spiritual history of Islam down the ages" (7). During the 2nd./8th and the 3rd./9th centuries, with the formation of the Shari'ah, discussed above, its guardians, the 'ulama' and the foqaha (religious scholars and jurists), who formed a kind of alliance with the administration, left aside the pious persons whose main interest was in spirituality rather than in the impersonal shari'ah. That was the final time of division between the orthodox Islam and the pious individuals. Referring to this point in the history of Islam, Dr. Fazlur Rahman says, "It was a reaction against this legal formulation of Islam—which was also its first formulated expression—that the early pietistic asceticism changed definitely into what is technically known as Sufism with its <u>propezethos</u>"(8). The Qur'anic concept of trust in God (<u>tawakkul 'ala Allah</u>), already emphasised by pietism in an ethical sense, was promoted in some places into an extreme dogma of renunciation of the world—a more serious cry than the prophetic exemplary life.

In the history of Sufism in Islam, there are two persons bearing the title <u>sufi</u>: Abu Hashim (d. 778 C. E.) and a well-known woman named Rabi'a (d. 801 C. E.) at Kufa and Basra, Iraq, respectively. Interestingly, the latter is well-known for discarding her marriage proposition with a man saying that she was in love with Allah and in fact married to Him (9). She is also reported to have said: "I love Thee with loves, love of my happiness. And perfect love, to love Thee, love of my happiness. And perfect love, to love Thee as is Thy due. My selfish love is that I do naught. But think on Thee, excluding all besides is but that purest love, which is Thy due, is that the veils which hide Thee fall, and I gaze on Thee. No praise to me in either this or that, nay, Thine the praise for path that love and this"(10).

It should be stated here that Islam as a complete system of life is individualistic, active and productive, as the Prophet Muhammad himself set the pattern, is not a pleasant place for the rise of mysticism (Sufism) which, by its very character or nature is ascetic in character—devotional and celibate and removed from social life in general. In this respect, there is a well-known saying attributed to the Prophet Muhammad: "There is no monasticism or monkery in Islam". With this saying on record, the rise of Sufism in Islam, is the direct result of Christian influence on Islam, since it conquered territories previously ruled by the Christian rulers, particularly in the Fertile Crescent (ancient Near-East), and also following the example of some individual Christians who converted to Islam. Islam also was influenced by Indian mysticism (Hindu-Buddhist) in Central

Asia, which the Muslims occupied in the middle of the 7th century C. E.

The first <u>sufis</u> had not predicted that one day they would come into disagreement with 'ulama and their allies and supporters—the Muslim administrative authorities. One of the crucial issues that the <u>sufis</u> were seriously concerned and outspoken about was "social justice" in general and particularly in their own community, as it was clear from the life of Hasan al-Basri. The relationship between the <u>sufis</u> and the administrative authorities was so unfriendly that the former never came close to the latter with the only exception of the Indian Naqshbandi order, when its head was Shaykh Ahmad Sirhindi. However, it was only to get the administration on their side to act in accord with the <u>sufi</u> wishes. The relationship of the <u>sufis</u> with the 'ulama (theologians/<u>fuqah'a</u>) was so hostile that the latter not only did not recognize any religious authority of the former but also openly and loudly declared them as hypocrites (<u>munafiq</u>) and "heterodox" (<u>ghayr-i-madhha</u>), particularly because of their concern with the intention (<u>niyya</u>) rather than with the outward performance (e. g. 'ibadat).

Nevertheless, ultimately the <u>sufis</u> organised themselves into orders and established their own "way" (<u>tariqah</u>) of religious—social life which was somehow different from the orthodox "way" (<u>Shari'ah</u>). Thus, the <u>Sufi</u> orders whose organizational foundation was like the pyramidal structure of the Catholic Christian priesthood eventually cut apart the "long-united <u>Ummah</u>" into two more or less hostile "ways", until al-Ghazzali reconciled them. Since then, they have promoted some friendly understanding between them.

Since the beginning, <u>sufis</u>, who extended their jurisdiction all over the Muslim world to carry out their mission of preaching and converting, began to incorporate ideas, words and practices from other religious orders fitting their mystical pursuit or goal, in addition to what was available in the Qur'an and the life of the Prophet Muhammad even before his prophethood, such as his meditative life, sometimes in the cave of Mount Hira, where he, in fact, received his first call to prophetic mission (nabuwwat: Q. 98). One of the well-known words the sufis began to use time and again, as early as the 3rd. century A. H. (9th century of the C. E.) is al-Haqq (The Real), the true God to Whom the sufi's soul aspires to be united with, "perhaps borrowed from the pseudo-theology of Aristotle", as suggested by L. Massionon, even though this word is found in many verses of the Qur'an (11). Since the Ghazzali's "rapprochement" between the Shari'ah and the Tariqah, the sufis also began to turn their attention to the Shari'ah vocabulary to borrow from it technical terms, whose sense they often slightly changed to suit their objectives. "Thus Shakik introduces tawakkul, Misri and Ibn Karran ma'rifa, Misri andBistami fana' (opp. Baqa", cf. Q. 55. 26f.). On the other side, whatever esoteric knowledge the sufis developed internally, they were coming forcefully under the influence of the Greco-Gnostic concepts and Christian and Manichaean doctrines. Thus a writer says, "An early example of the intrusion into Sufism (later 3rd. 9th century) of these Gnostic-Manichaean ideas was the doctrine of Muhammad as the Prime Light, the penultimate constituent of ontological reality after God, a doctrine which later became a centrally 'orthodox' doctrine of Sufism through the teaching of Ibn al-'Arabi (7th/13th century) who had made of this light God Himself". "With the doctrine of Muhammad as the Prime Light in which all the prophets were foreshadowed, including Adam, emerged the Hadith . . . , which declared that Muhammad was a Prophet while Adam was still (in a state) between water and earth"(12).

From our aforesaid study of Sufism's origins and the success, it is abundantly clear that there is a combination of both indigenous as well as foreign elements. Naturally, it is historically untenable to hold that <u>Sufism</u> as a whole is a system of foreign origin, as the earlier studies thought. However, from the beginning of Islam, it can be pointed out that the formation of the ideas special to <u>Sufism</u> went on from within in the course of attentive and diligent recitations of and meditations on the Qur'an and <u>Hadith</u>, under the influence of social and individual cries in the real centre of the Muslim Community (<u>ummat al-muslimin</u>). Nevertheless, Massignon says: ". . . if the initial framework of Sufism was specifically Muslim and Arab, it is not exactly useless to identify the foreign decorative elements which came to be added to this framework and flourish there; in this way it has been possible for recent students to discover several devotional elements derived from Christian monachism . . . and several Greek philosophical terms translated from the Syriac; the Iranian analogies . . . as to the Indian elements . . . few arguments have been added to the old similar conjectures of al-Beruni and Dara Shikuh on the parallels between the Upanishads or the Yoga Sutra and the ideology of primitive Sufism"(13).

In a nutshell, despite the fact that <u>Sufism</u> is fundamentally Islamic, nevertheless, during the course of its gradual development, particularly in formulating its final doctrine and organisation into orders, it did absorb some elements from all those non-Arab countries where the <u>sufis</u> went following the Muslim army, and engaged themselves as preachers in the absence of a priestly class.

Having gone through the steps of development and completion of ideas, <u>Sufism</u> came to be a movement not completely bound by the <u>Shari'ah</u> rules. Its partial freedom from following the <u>Shari'ah</u>, in its later stages, allowed some <u>sufis</u> to adopt both an attitude of freedom towards Islam as a total system of life, on the one hand, and a liberal attitude towards other religions, on the other. Thus a writer says, <u>Sufism</u> is something "which essentially is not a system based on authority and tradition, but a free movement assuming infinitely various forms in obedience to the inner light of the individual soul" (14).

While discussing <u>sufi</u> liberalism, it should be stated that since the 5th/11th century onward, <u>Sufi</u> orders started preaching openly and mixed with the peoples of non-Semitic religions, for example Hindus, Buddhists and perhaps Jains on the Indian subcontinent. From that inter-communication, <u>Sufism</u> began to develop multifarious tendencies and to assimilate more and more foreign (non-Islamic) ideas, which the <u>Sufi</u> orders incorporated into their social-religious life. The extent of flow of non-Islamic ideas into <u>Sufism</u> had so much impact that in the long run it was considered as roughly divided into orthodox (<u>ba-shara'</u>) and heterodox (<u>be-shara'</u>)—conforming to orthodox Islam and not conforming to orthodox Islam—respectively. Incidentally, this division was seen applicable particularly to non-Semitic countries like India and Africa, especially the former, where a new heterodox mystic movement facilitated through the interaction of Hindu-Muslim ideas was born, well-known as the Bhakti movement, promoted by Kabir (1440-1518), the Bhakta, influenced the entire sub-continent of the present-day Bangladesh, India and Pakistan, generating a large group of sub-orders named Kabir-<u>Panthis</u> (15). In this context, referring specially to the Indian sub-continent where <u>Sufism</u> became "eclectic and syncretic", Dr. Fazlur Rahman says, ". . . the Indian subcontinent teems with a host of questionable and so-called 'irregular' (<u>be-shara'</u>) orders which are . . . very loosely organized and, as their name implies, are not bound either by discipline or by the religious law of Islam. In this sub-continent, Muslim religious life, at a popular level, has been profoundly influenced by indigenous beliefs and practices; or, rather, the local Muslim population, despite its conversion to Islam, has largely kept its pre-Islamic <u>Weltansehauung</u> alive . . . The conversion has been purely nominal and the process of Islamization has been a painfully slow one—so strong is the influence of spiritual romanticism to which the native population had ever been prey"(16). It should also be mentioned here that Kabir's Bhakti was not only a be-shara' Sufi order, it also claimed itself as "supra-denominational Sufism" which asked for the unification of Hinduism and Islam on the Bhakti level. For sure, it is well-known that in some villages Hindus and Muslims worshipped common saints, e. g. panj pir (five saints). This was the direct long-period result of the well-known "rapprochment" between Hinduism and Islam on the Indian subcontinent of those days effective as from the "Brahmanabad Charter of 712 C. E. (17). On the other hand, the influence of Islamic monotheism on Hinduism resulted in the birth of a new religion, viz., Sikhism, a mixture of the two religions, founded by Guru Nanak, a disciple of Kabir. Equally, Indonesia, where Islam reached not before the 12th century C. E., had not adequate time to establish firmly its compact before Portuguese colonialism reached there. As a result, many of the religious activities of the Muslim population remain basically un-Islamic beneath the exterior. "Besides, therefore, a leavening of the Muslim orders that have made their way there, the pre-Islamic mystic attitudes remain almost unchanged" (18).

Since it is well-known that Sufism won its greatest achievement on the continent of Bangladesh, India and Pakistan (the present situation)—the land of former polytheism, and later, atheism in the form of Buddhism and Jainism—we proceed to discuss the history of Sufism there, for it is the greatest single territory for the rise and spread of Sufism. There were some particular sufis who came into direct contact with both Hindu and Buddhist ideas in India. The earliest contact between Sufism and Buddhism took place in the 8th century C. E. in the north-western Persian and Central Asian marshes where Hindu-Buddhist ideas had been widely known before the conquest of Islam in the 8th century C. E. King Ashoka, who adopted Buddhist Binaya Pitaka, propagated that lesson in Sri Lanka and also in the Central Asian region including Iran or Persia. "In about 259 B. C., Ashoka took the momentous resolution of organizing a network of preaching mission to spread the teaching of the Buddha, not only throughout India but in the distant regions of Western Asia, Eastern Europe, and North Africa"(19). It is also reported that Khalid, the wazir (minister) of the Abbasid Caliph al-Mansur, was the son of a Barmak (chief priest) in a Buddhist monastery in Balkh, called Nowbahar. R. A. Nicholson tells about those "flourishing Buddhist monasteries in Balkh, the metropolis of ancient Bactaria, a city famous for the number of Sufis who resided in it" (20). Another famous author on this subject, Ignaz Goldziher, tells about the wonderful conditions in what the Sufi ascetic Ibrahim ibn Adham, a prince of Balkh, who abandoned his throne and adopted the life of a "wandering mendicant—the story of Buddha all over again"(21). Interestingly, Goldziher too makes analogies between the "noble path of Buddhism" and "Path" (tariqa) of Sufism; between the Sufi "concentration" (muraqaba) and the Buddhist "dhayana" (22). The same famous writer also thinks that the sufi interpretation of Divine Unity (tawhid) is not basically different from the Islamic monotheistic conception of God, possibly borrowed from Indian theosophy (23). Sufi robes and the use of rosaries are also considered to have been borrowings from Buddhism. Thus, C. Nicholson says: "The Sufis learned the use of rosaries from Buddhist monks and, without entering into the details, it may be safely asserted that the method of Sufism, so far as it is one of the ethical self-culture, ascetic meditation, and intellectual abstraction, owes a good deal to Buddhism"(24).

From the aforesaid discussion, it has become abundantly clear that Sufism adopted a very liberal policy not only with regard to Islam but also to other religions, including Hinduism and Buddhism; as a result, it easily absorbed elements from those religious systems. That liberal policy eventually created a division in Sufism into orthodox and heterodox—the latter was open to any ideas, thus absorbed freely.

Now, let us deal with some individual <u>sufis</u> who are well-known for their multi-religious practices on the Indian subcontinent, in particular: The first <u>sufi</u> who is known to have been influenced "fundamentally by Indian mystical ideas was Abu Yazid Bistami"(d. 261/875), a <u>sufi</u> well-known to have learned some Indian ideas from his <u>guru</u> (religious or mystical teacher), Abu 'Ali Sindhi (of Sindh). For instance, the conception of Divine Unity and <u>fana</u> (passing away), which appears at Bistami's discussions, has been explained as derivative of Vedic and Buddhist origin. Thus Nicholson emphatically says, "The Sufi conception of the passing away (<u>fana</u>) of the individual self in Universal Being, is certainly, I think, Indian. Its first great exponent was the Persian mystic, Bayzid of Bistam, who may have received it from his teacher [<u>guru</u>], Abu 'Ali of Sindh . . ."(25).Nonetheless, A. J. Arberry does not agree with the above opinion and proposes that the <u>sufi</u> got the idea of <u>fana</u> from the Qur'anic verse: "Everything upon the earth (<u>appsath</u>) passes away save His face"(55. 26f.) (26).

However, Zaehner suggests that Abu Yazid was influenced by Shankara Vedanta because in one of his sayings, Abu Yazid is reported to have said that God told him, "O Abu Yazid, verily my creation longs to see thee". And I said: "Adorn me with Thy Unity and clothe me in Thine I-ness and raise me up into Thy Oneness, so that when Thy creatures see me, they may say: "We have seen thee (i. e. God) and Thou art That" (27). Obviously, this is the well-known Sanskrit phrase: <u>tat tawam asi</u> ("Thou art That") used for Brahman and <u>Atman</u>—Universal Self and individual self-respectively—as synonyms (28). Moreover, Bistami once said, "I went from God to God, until they cried from me in me, 'O Thou I!'" Commenting on this verse, Nicholson says, "This, it would be observed, is not Buddhism, but the pantheism of the Vedanta"(29). It is said by well-known writers that the Sufi theory of fana was influenced to some extent by Buddhism as well as by "Perso-Indian Pantheism"(30).

Judging all the well-known sayings of Bistami, it is reasonable to conjecture that Bistami must have gone through a mystical experience during which he must have felt himself to be one with God. "And it was this overpowering sensation of being rapt into the Godhead that caused him to utter such blasphemies, so detestable to the orthodox, as his notorious 'subhani!maa'zama shani' (Glory be to Me! How great is My majesty"(31). Notwithstanding the above information, Bistami did not renounce Islam. He even performed hajj (pilgrimage) a few times.

We have discussed above that the Indian ideas that fashioned Bistami's mystical life. In confirmation of this fact, one writer says, Bistami "injected into the body of Sufism a dose of Indian Vedanta that was soon to transform the whole movement. It was now within the power of every Sufi to realise himself as God, and this entitled him to live in total disregard of Muslim religious law"(32). Another writer says that Bayzid's saying established in Sufism the Indian Vedantic concept of absolute monism (33).

Another famous non-orthodox sufi, al-Husayn ibn Mansur, known as al-Hallaj ('the wool carder': d. 309/922), used much stronger language (disliked by orthodox Muslims), than Bistami and shook the whole Muslim world by his un-Islamic ideas: "The man who produced the greatest stir in the Islamic world, by the boldness of his doctrines was Husayn bin Mansur al-Hallaj"(34). However, his theories were later developed or worked up by many famous sufis (35).

It is reported that Hallaj went to India (Sind, Pakistan) to study Indian magic, and wrote a few books on it. He was treated as a heretic when he began teaching as an apostle. He was captured and was ultimately executed by the 'Abbasid government (36). According to Hallaj's theory of creation, the absolute God in His divinity (lahut) became in Adam God in humanity (nasut). Thus, considering Adam as the manifestation of God, Hallaj conceived of this relation of God with man as the infusion of the divine into the human—a reference to the emanatory theory of creation that is found in the Qur'an (15. 29) as well as in Brihat.Up. 1. 4.7 and in many other Indian (Hindu) religious texts (37).

Moreover, it is also a clear reference to the birth of Jesus as a spirit of Allah infused into the womb of Mary, as it is mentioned in the Qur'an (3. 45, 47). In fact, Hallaj considered Jesus as the perfect kind of deified man (insan-ul-kamil), but rejected by Islam, who is the Prophet of Allah on earth born of Mary. Moreover, the union of lahut and nasut, thinks Hallaj, called hulul (incarnation), is also unacceptable to Islam. In other words, God incarnates Himself on earth through the perfect man, as Jesus is to Christianity. The incarnation is explained as the commixture (imtizaz) of the divine and human nature (38). Finally, Hallaj applied the doctrine of commixture to himself in the following words: "I am He whom I love, and whom I loved is I. We are two spirits dwelling in one body. If thou seest me, thou seest us both" (39). And in his extreme ecstasy, Hallaj declared: "Ana'l-Haqq"(I am the Haqq or Truth, that is, God). Notwithstanding Hallaj was perhaps the most radical of all sufis, nevertheless, his ideas were integrated into the system of Sufism, although rejected by Islam. It goes without saying that Hallaj undoubtedly demonstrated the highest degree of sufi liberalism, yet he performed the hajj, like an orthodox Muslim.

Sufis borrowed Indian religious ideas with their extreme liberalism even towards a non-Semitic religious tradition or system. Apart from the Indian Bhakta-Kabir, there was another person, named, Abu Sa'id ibn Abi'l Khayr (d. 440/1049) of Khurasan, who not only spoke against some of the external requirements of Islam such as Prayer, Fasting and Pilgrimage, but also urged for unification of faith and infidelity.

It should be stated emphatically that Abu Sa'id's ideas are not, in fact, a rejection of Islam per se; quite the opposite, the rejection was meant only for the external forms of religion. To the sufis, for sure, the essence of religion is not the formal act but the "annihilation" or "passing away" from self into the Divine attributes and qualities (99 names of Allah) which is achieved in "ecstasy". Their position is that the formal religion is only for the beginners in the way of God, and those mystics who have already reached the final stage of their spiritual journey towards the Truth (God), now live in eternal communication with God. Hence one writer says, "Those who have seen the radiant vision of the Divine, protest against the exaggerated importance attached to outward form" (4o). It may be pointed out that at this stage, they are above formal requirements rather than against them. This is just another point of sufi liberalism.

It is also important to mention here that "conterminous with the sufi concept of fana is wilaya" (sainthood) which was elaborated with an appeal to the use of the word wali' ('friend of God'), "but with a peculiar Sufi content borrowed from mysticism of Eastern Christianity, Gnosticism and later on from Neoplatonism"(41).

In passing, it may be mentioned that the concept of sainthood also brought with it the doctrine of hierarchy of 'preserving' saints. This theory, after all, led the sufis being organised in a pyramidal structure, each rung of it is under a qutb (pillar-saint), and on the top of the whole structure is the <u>qutb-ul-aqtab</u> (the chief saint of the Pillar-Saints), around which (structure) the whole universe rotates. This structure was parallel to the Shi'ah doctrine of the <u>Imam</u> (leader) which was a borrowing from the Christian priestly structure: the Pope=(<u>Qutb-ul-aqtab</u>). "A special place in a Sufi hierarchy is occupied by an invisible figure called al-khadir or al-khidr (literary the Green) who, like the Phoenix, even recreates his Youth, is immortal, and whose chief function is to guide those who lose their way in the wilderness (both physical and spiritual)" (42).

It may be mentioned here that saint worship, probably a universal phenomenon, passing from civilization to civilization, affected even the monotheistic Islam through <u>be-shara'</u> <u>Sufism</u>. Hence Maurice Gaudefroy-Demombynes says: "Buddhism and Christianity, although they brought man nearer to sheltering divinity, . . . , have not escaped any more than iconoclasting Islam, from the worship of saints and relics." "The sanctuaries of Islamic saints occupied the sites as ancient holy places; water springs, trees, stones, hill tops, which had already been chosen for their dwelling places by the ancient gods and saints of Jews and Christians"(43). Eventually, belief in miracles of the saints became so popular that miracle mongering combined with the spiritual "demagogy" of many <u>sufi-saints</u> opened the door for all sorts of growths or accretions, including charlatanism. Miraculous power was considered <u>baraka</u> or blessing (<u>fayd</u>). By the way, the widespread belief in this <u>Baraka</u> resulted in popular veneration of saints, tombs and other relics. Progressively, celebrating '<u>urs</u> (pilgrimage to saints' shrines) became a well-known and practised event for all people irrespective of their religious beliefs and practices.

Ultimately, the personality of the <u>sufi shaykh</u> (saints) became so powerful and "mind-arresting" weapon or tool that <u>Sufism</u> became practically a 'cult of personalities'. "The term be-pira 'guideless person' became almost equivalent to godless person"(44).

Following the above-mentioned development, Sufism moved away from its practical life to the visionary field. Hence, for practical purposes, Sufi circles went through 'metempsychosis'. As one critic blames, "Instead of being a method of moral self-discipline and elevation and genuine spiritual enlightenment, Sufism was now transformed into variable spiritual jugglery through auto-hypnotic transports and divisions just as at the level of doctrine it was being transmuted into a half-delirious theosophy"(45). All the sufis we have discussed above were unorthodox rather than kafir (disbelievers). The case of Kabir, it should be emphasised, was unprecedented for the fact that it took the responsibility of a unique task—the union of the two fundamentally different systems of religions, viz., Hinduism and Islam—polytheism and monotheism respectively. That liberal attitude was deeply implanted in Indo-Islamic culture and resulted from the interaction of the two diametrically opposed religions.

Now let us discuss Sufism as a missionary movement in India and elsewhere. To begin with, sufi teaching and preaching individually as well as in groups, created an atmosphere of tolerance and understanding between Hinduism and Islam. It should be stressed that their simple message of peace, equality and brotherhood, sharing with and caring for, if converted to Islam, the sufis attracted to them, in particular, the Hindu lower classes: "That message, . . . , worked like a magic power in a caste-ridden society—for the untouchables in particular" (46). In this context, it is said, where the Muslim soldiers conquered the Indian territories, the sufis actually conquered the hearts of the Indian people—the untouchables, in particular. Commending the sufi contribution to the spread of Islam, in general, one writer says that Islam as a religion scored its greatest success through the Sufis and not through the help of the political rules. Needless to say, sufi propagation of Islam produced the "most lasting missionary triumphs" (47). Another writer goes further and says, "In the process of conquests and Islamisation, the Muslim preachers, the Sufis, not the soldiers, emphasised not on the Unity of God against many local divinities of the conquered lands, e. g. India and Africa in particular, but also on the humanity of the Islamic message such as the equality of men, a global community of brotherhood of believers, sharing-caring, dignity of women, etc." (48). This type of message worked like fire in India—a caste-ridden society, and in Africa, a society of social inequality because of the tribal system and "widespread animism". Some of the local Sudanese traders, especially, would feel that to become Muslims would raise them in social status; and the African animistic religions could mean little to traders who were moving about, since each could be practised in the home village. In the Indian context, it was mostly the results of sufi missionary works that created what is popularly known "Indian Islam" (49). It is also well-known that the appearance of the sufis on the Indian soil resulted in an atmosphere of peace and goodwill because they were different from Muslim conquerors. In this regard, we are told about one of the Sufi Shaykhs, named Shaykh Isma'il, whose sermon at Lahore brought together a large number of Hindus, and no one of them came in personal contact with him without converting to Islam. It should be mentioned here that geographic-historian, Baladhuri, tells us that during the three hundred years of Arab rule in Sindh, there were Many Hindus, including several princes who converted to Islam (50).

The name of another top-ranking sufi should be mentioned because of his outstanding contributions. It was Pir Sadr-ud-Din who went to Sindh (now in Pakistan) in the thirties of the 15th century C. E., and demonstrated the Sufi principle of liberalism to the extent that he was reported to have taken a Hindu name (not available to this writer). Undoubtedly, he just wanted to have a name like those of his audience—the Hindus. Over and above, he is also reported to have written a book, entitled Dasavatara ("Tenth Incarnation") in which the khalifa "'Ali is designated to be the tenth incarnation of Vishnu. He is also reported to have accepted the nine Hindu incarnations of Vishnu as real. He is also reported to have identified Brahma with the Prophet Muhammad and Adam with Shiva (51).

There were some other sufis who carried out their mission, prosylytisation, peacefully all over India, particularly in the northern and western parts of it. They not only converted to Islam a large number of Hindus but also some tribes, for instance, the Ravuttans of Madura, Tinneuvelly, Coimbatore, and some more (52). In South India, the case of the Lingayata-Vira Shaiva headed by Basava, who abandoned all elements of Hinduism, under the Sufi influence, except the Shiva Linga worship (whence the name Lingayata), is well-known to be one of the best achievements of Sufi missionary work in India.(53).

Of the most renowned Sufis of north and north-western India, the most distinguished were Khawajah Mu'in-ud-Din Chisti of Ajmir (d. 1236 C. E.), Khawajah Qutb-ud-Din Bakhtiyar Kaki of Delhi (d. 12 36), Nizam ud-Din Awliya of Delhi (d. 1356) and Nasir-ud-Din Chirag-i-Delhi (d. 1356) who made important contributions to the propagation of Islam on the Indian sub-continent by exercising Sufi liberalism, thus, Islamic liberalism and humanism. Their followers came from every walk of life of the then Indian society in large numbers. Their major message was Unity of God and Love for Him, the equality of man and social justice. Thus, the spiritual policy of the Sufis was sulh-i-kul (peace with all). That policy resulted not only in the conversion of people but also in the creation of some small communities such as the Husayni Brahmins of Rajputana and the Muslim Rajputs of Panipath—they were actually a mixture of the two faiths, as their names say. Thus, Baghi says, "The period between 1200-1500 was remarkable for the permeation of Sufis throughout India. New sects and movements arose midway between Hinduism and Islam . . . There were mass conversions to Islam under the spell of Sufis. To make Islam emotionally satisfying, they made several concessions to the practices of their creeds" (54).

It may be pointed out here that to the sufis, all religions are true in essence. For instance, Shabistari, a Persian sufi, is reported to have said that Sufis are ever ready to accept what is good in other religions, like idol-worship, fire-worship, etc. : "Idol worship is essentially unification" (55). That is to say, in his opinion, idol worship as a manifestation of God cannot be evil.

About the question of Divine Love, Ibn al-'Arabi (d. 1240) said that no religion is more majestic than a religion of love and longing for God. Love is the essence of all religions: the true mystic welcomes it in whatever language or motion it may assume. The poem below, attributed to him, tells clearly the type of liberalism a sufi wants towards all religion:

"My heart has become capable of every form:
It is a posture for Gazelles and a convent for Christian monks,
And a temple for idols, and the pilgrims' ka'ba,
And the Tables of the Tora and the book of Koran.
I follow the religion of Love, whichever way his camels take.
My religion and my faith is the true religion.
We have a pattern in Bishr, the lover of Hind her sister, and
In Qays and Lubna, and Mayya and Ghaylan"(56).

It may be mentioned here that one of the most outspoken advocates of the liberal sufi attitude was the famous Amir Khusreau, who referred to Hindu customs and ceremonies in a mind of cordiality which must have been responsible for discovering the fundamental truth of basic unity between Hinduism and Islam. Thus, he is reported to have said:

"Though Hindu is not faithful like me,
He often believes in the same thing as I do" (57).

That was the type of tolerance <u>sufis</u> had even towards a polytheistic system like Hinduism. Therefore, they did not find it difficult to establish friendly relationships with the Hindus even by a give-and-take attitude towards some customs and practices. For that kind of liberal policy, they were respected by both Muslims and Hindus equally, and at death, their tombs and shrines were venerated by both communities and visited as places of pilgrimage ('<u>urs</u>). It is in this respect that some <u>sufis</u> adopted the Hindu ideal of <u>ahimsa</u> (non-injury/violence), thus, became vegetarian, e. g. Shaykh Hamid-ud-Din Nagori and his disciples. The <u>Sufi</u> culture influenced the Indian culture so much that there was a general rapprochement on all levels including intermarriage with simple conversion of Hindu women.

On the other hand, Indian or Hindu influence on the Muslims was increasingly heavy; for example, simple, thus imperfect, conversion allowed the new Muslims—men and women to retain a large portion of their customs and practices. Thus, while the new Muslims in general created a mixed Indo-Islamic body politic, the new Muslim wives, specifically those who married the <u>Sufis</u>, established mixed Indo-Islamic families wherein, because of mother's greater role in raising a family, Hindu elements played greater role, for example, in all family activities, including birth, marriage and death ceremonies (58). By the way, in <u>sufi</u> families there is no divorce or widow remarriage, as in Hindu families. Interestingly, unlike any other Muslim, Indian Muslims, contrary to the well-known Islamic principles of equality and brotherhood, under the Hindu influence considered society as consisting of four main classes: namely, "men of the pen, men o the sword, men of business and men of the soil". The first is the guardian of religion and learning; the second is the guardian of the first, and the third and fourth are the sustainers of the first and second. Any attempt to upset the order of the family can only lead to chaos and confusion.

In another social-religious practice, the Hindu guru-chela relationship has become the pir-murid relationship in the Sufi community. Interestingly, dhikr (devotional recitation of Allah's names and attributes) is a regular Sufi practice (cf. Q. 76. 25; 33. 41). But the process and method of dhikr is similar to the meditation and breathing exercises of Yoga, and for this reason, possibly, some yogis were attached to sufis, like Farid-ud-Din Ganj-i-Shakar, Nizam-ud-Din Awliya and some others (59). It should be pointed out here that some Sufi orders such as the Shatari accepted yogic elements and used to live in jungles, like the yogis, and because of their wandering habits, they were called the "qalandars". Sufis also built khanqas (mystic's cottage) which is equal to the Buddhist bihara (monastery). That is to say that following the Buddhist tradition, some sufis practised monasticism.

Religiously (theologically), although Islam does not allow sama' and ginna (singing and dancing accompanied by music), nevertheless, following the local customs, Sufi orders introduced singing and dancing with music in halaqa (Sufi circles) on the then Indian subcontinent as well as outside of it. Imam Ghazzali called them bid'at (innovations), nevertheless, gave the green signal as fruitful for the Sufis as they "stir up in themselves greater love towards God" (60). On the sub-continent of the present day Bangladesh, India and Pakistan (alphabetically), at least four well-known orthodox orders, viz., Qadiriya, Naqshbandiya Chishtiya and Suhrawardiya are practising sama' with enthusiasm and call it Qawwali, and is equated with the Hindu devotional song (kirtan). Hence, Tarachand says, "Sufism indeed was a religion of intense devotion; love was its passion; poetry, song and dance its worship, and passing away in God its ideal"(61).

Some rural sufis joined the Hindus "in venerating and worshipping" some well-known heroes like Ghazi Mijan, Pir Badr, Khawajah Khizr, (whose Muslim name was Hinduised into Rajah Kidr), Panj Pir, Guga or Zahir Pir and Satya Pir, they, surprisingly, were the Hindu-Muslim common gods.

Another significant common aspect of Sufi liberalism was their interest in learning the local languages of every country or region wherever they went in pursuit of their missionary work, as the Christian missionary did. In North India, for instance, they evolved a common medium for the exchange of ideas, called the Hindi or Hidustani language, and Bhakta Kabir is regarded as the father of the Hindi literature.(62).

Interestingly, some Indian sufis also took serious interest in Hindu literary works. Some of their works are very interesting. For example, The Prophets of India: Rama and Krishna, Peace be on them, by Hasan Nizami, a descendent of Nizam-ud-Din Awliya. The author maintains that according to the Qur'an (cf. 16. 36), God sent His messengers (paygambars) in all parts of the world. How can then India be excepted? Therefore, Rama, Krishna and Buddha are all the apostles of India and their teachings cannot be false or invalid. Undoubtedly, this is probably one of the best examples of Sufi broadmindedness particularly in the field of religion.

In our above-mentioned subject, we mentioned that the interaction between Hindu-Muslim ideas on the Sufistic level was very friendly and mutual. Emphasising on this point, Titus says, "If the Indian environment has produced a profound effect on Islam during its long residence in the country, it is no less true that Islam has in turn reacted on Hinduism and Indian life" (63). That is to say, while the pre-Sufi Muslim India was one of prejudice and mistrust, the post-Sufi Muslim India was made into a pleasant place for both communities conditioned by Sufi humanism and liberalism. The environment of understanding and sense of respect for one another in matters of life, generated by the peaceful "Sufi propagation", made it possible for the Muslim minority to rule over a Hindu-majority India for over a thousand years. In a nutshell, when the non-Sufi-Muslims (orthodox) with their dogmatic-minded attitudes failed to face the peculiar situation in a "polytheistic-atheistic" country, as India is, the Sufis "rose to the occasion and released syncretic forces which liquidated social, ideological and linguistic berriers" between the two communities, as mentioned above, "and helped in the development of a common cultural outlook" (64). By the way, that culture is widely known as the Indo-Islamic culture, somewhat different from the Islamic culture in other countries and places. Hence, commenting on the whole range of the situation resulting from the interaction between the two communities affecting almost all affairs of their lives, Sir John Marshall describes the picture in these words: "Seldom in the history of mankind has the spectacle been witnessed of two civilizations, so vast and so strangely developed, yet so radically dissimilar, as the Muhammadan and the Hindu, meeting and mingling together. The very contrast which existed between them, the wide divergence of their culture and their religion, make the history of their impact peculiarly instructive"(65).

However, the long-term interaction had long-term consequences: that interaction resulted in inter-absorption, thus assimilation, which was too much for Islam to bear or to tolerate. As a result, two religious reform movements were launched almost simultaneously in Eastern Bengal and North India. Although the "assimilation" was two-way phenomenon, nonetheless the growth or accretion, particularly from Hinduism to Islam, resulted in unacceptable aberrations. Naturally, in order to purge or reform Islam of Hindu elements, Al-Hajj Shari'atullah started the Fara'idi Movement in the former place in the early days of the nineteenth century (beginning in 1802) (66).

It should be mentioned that later in the same century, another reform movement (I call it the "Mujahidin Movement", but wrongfully known as the "Wahhabi Movement" by W. W. Hunter in his book entitled:The Indian Musalman) was started in the later part of the above-mentioned century by Sayyid Ahmad of Ra'I Berli (1201-1246/1786-1831). Both reform movements, it should be mentioned, were inspired and invigorated by Neo-Sufism, viz., the Tariqah'-I Muhammadiyah (The Way of the Prophet) (67).

In addition to what is discussed above, there were other countries where sufis played an active role in displaying their natural spirit of understanding and accommodation, as on the Indian subcontinent. It should be stated clearly that the Muslim army, to begin with, did not conquer all the lands that formed what is called the Muslim World even to the present time. sufis always followed the Muslim army to preach Sufism out of their missionary zeal, in the newly conquered lands, completely independent of the latter. Before the sufis, Muslim traders, who carried out "missionary" works as well, also married newly converted Muslim ladies, who retained a great deal of their pre-Islamic customs and practices. "And when the Sufis appeared on the scene, they replaced the traders in their missionary activities, and, of course, continued the practice of marriage with the aforesaid consequences"(68).

It should be stated here that Sufism got itself involved in non-missionary activities such as the social-political affairs of the Umma. In addition to these, its opposition towards orthodox Islam increasingly became powerful and bold. In addition to that, in its efforts to be more effective and popular, it appealed to the public. In Turkey, for example, <u>Sufi</u> organisation had been associated with many anti-government rebellions since the 13th century to the 17th century; the case of Shaykh Baba Ilyas during the Saljuq rule was famous.

In addition to their pure religious activities, they were also involved in social-religious activities such as <u>Sufi sama'</u> with music in countries like India, a typical Hindu practice. The Naqshbandi order, for example, used both <u>dhikr</u> and <u>sama'</u> with music and noisy or wild dancing also in Turkey. By the way, this order spread to Central Asia as well, China, the Malaysian Archipelago and practised its normal culture. There were still some strange and wild orders whose dancing "was accompanied by the rending of garments and other 'mystical' feats such as eating glass (practices which have been attributed to the Shamanistic influences brought by the Mongol invasion"(69).

In Turkey, the oldest <u>Sufi</u> order was the Yasawiya with Shamanistic background which was transmitted to its branch, the Bektashiya of the 12th century. It is known to have been the most popular boorish or clumsy order there. "The Bektashiya, besides conserving Shamanistic elements, developed Shi'ite trends on the one hand, and some Christian beliefs and practices, on the other; these latter are said to have been imbibed by them from the already existing background of the territories through which they spread. Thus, they not only believe in the twelve Shi'ite Imams but also make a trinity out of God, Muhammad and 'Ali"(70). As a matter of fact, following the Christian practice, they admit a new member consuming wine, cheese and bread, as in Albania, "and confess their sins to their spiritual guides who grant them absolution. Among the established orders, the Bektashiya are the furthest removed from orthodoxy, caring little for the obligatory law of Islam"(71).

It should be stated here that the Mawlayia order in Turkey, founded by the well-known Persian Sufi-poet, Mawlana Jalaluddin Rumi (d. 1273) also practised dancing in a circle so violently that the Mawlawiyas came to be widely known "the dancing dervishes" or "the whirling/howling dervishes".

Another widely known orthodox order, was the Qadiriya, also known to have practised dancing and music along with other physical movements. A younger contemporary of Qadiriya was the Rifa'iya (12th century) which had spread into Iraq, Egypt, Turkey and some parts of South-East Asia, used extravagant forms of dhikr and other rituals borrowed from other countries it went into. In Egypt, there was another "rustic" order named the Badawiya which indulged in local popular practices such as star-watching and not talking to people normally or for long time.

In north-west Africa, the spread of Islam with a political message was carried out in association with sufis. During the 12th century, the Al-Muwahhidin (Almohad Dynasty), succeeded the Al-Murabitun (Almoravids), who carried on an orthodox jihad movement of Islamisation in the 11th century. Some orders, such as the 'Isawiya of Morocco in the 15th century, practised the sword-slashing ritual—an adoption from local animism (72).

As we have studied so far, Sufism, using its spiritual liberalism, carried out its missionary works in the continents of Asia and Africa successfully. Incidentally, it allowed its converts to retain some elements of their previous tradition, which perverted Islam. So, Fazlur Rahman says, "Within its latitudinariarism, latent in it from the beginning, it allowed a motley of religious attitudes inherited by the new converts from their previous backgrounds, from animism in Africa to pantheism in India"(73). This strong mentality to compromise with local ideas and practices of the new converts has divided the united Islam into several religious groups. In the Maghrib (North-west Africa), especially, "Through popular Sufism, Berbar and African animistic beliefs and rituals have imposed their own form on Islam in Africa; the 'marabout' (murabit) of the Berbers, the 'holy man' or 'religious leader' (the alfa) of the Negro Muslim is basically a carry-over from the pre-Islamic cults of holy men and witch doctors of Negro fetishism. In its expansion through Central Africa, Islam came into close contact with the similar animistic cult of Shamanism"(74).

It should be stated emphatically that notwithstanding the above-mentioned characteristics of Sufism, by virtue of liberalism and compromise, Sufism has converted millions of people within the banner of Islam with wonderful rapidity, and up to the present time is still a "proselytizing force in Africa", especially where Islam is the fastest growing system of religion.

In Western Africa, following the conquest of the Fertile Crescent during the thirties of the 7th century, the northern Central Asia and the Caucasious regions were converted to Islam by the sufis. "In those heterogeneous regions, Sufistic Islam became the only unifying force. There were, and still are, three main ethnic groups, namely, the Turks, the Iranians and the Ibero-Caucasians"(75).

The Central Asia-Caucasian region is one of the most important blocks of the Muslim World (76). All signs of pre-Islamic civilizations (Buddhist, Mamebean and Nestorian) have disappeared, but the sufis absorbed local elements, as in other places. The orders which worked tirelessly in these physically difficult regions were the Naqshbandiya and the Qadiriya. By the eighth century, Eastern

Transcaucasia (now Azarbayjan) became predominantly a Muslim country (with some Jews and Christians living together peacefully) because of sufi propagation. In this region, it should be pointed out, that because of sufi liberalism, a multi-ethnic population such as a mixed Iranean-Iberic and Turkish Saljuks, live in total harmony and peace, similarly Daghestan. Although the Muslim army conquered this Central Caucasus region in the seventh century, yet it was only in the late sixteenth century that it adopted Islam because of the Naqhbandi and Qadiri Sufi preaching. The same is true about the Chechens who were converted to Islam by the Sufi orders sometime in the eighteenth century. "Like Central Asia, the Caucasus is an extraordinary mosaic of races and languages where Sufistic Islam is the only unifying force" (77). The present situation, there is still the same. As a matter of fact, the whole region, north of the Black Sea, is predominantly a Muslim area since the fourteenth century as a result of the Sufi "proselytysing works—policy of sulh-i-kul (peace with all") (78).

To conclude the present issue: We have seen that "Neo-Sufism" appeared on the scene as early as the time of Shaykh Ahmad Sirhindi (d.1625) who led the campaign for the purification of Sufism on the Indian subcontinent, followed by other reform movements. The same type of reformation activities were also carried out in the Muslim Maghrib in the 12th century by the Al-Muwahhidin, who, under the leadership of Mahdi ibn Tumart continued the earlier purification movement of Al-Murabitin. The same purificational movement was also carried out by the Sanusiya in Libya where Italian colonialism was finished by the Sanusiya government.

Hence, after a few hundred years of struggle for the unification of the Shari'ah and the Tariqah, including al-Ghazzali's efforts to that end, the two ways of the Muslim religious life eventually united under the Tariqah'-i-Muhammadiyah opening the way to become a united Islam again. Referring to this historical phenomenon, Dr. Fazlur Rahman says, "It provides us with a shining example of that fundamentally catholic genius of Islam—a panoroma of continued tensions and challenges and of equally persistent efforts to resolve those tensions and meet those challenges in a process of modification, adaptation and absorption" (79). Thus, liberalism and rationalism are inherent in Islam.

CHAPTER 6 : References

1. Cf. Massignon, "Tasawwuf", Shorter Encyclopaedia of Islam (SEI); also cf. Stewart, P. J., Unfolding Islam, 1st. ed., Ithaca Press, U. K., 1994, pp. 175ff.
2. Waddy, C., The Muslim Mind, Longman, London, 1976, p. 151.
3. Evelyn, Underhill, Introduction to the Autobiography of Maharshi Devendranath Tagore, tr. Satyendranath Tagore and Indira Devi from original Bengali, London, 1914, p.X1.
4. Sufism: An Account of the Mystics of Islam, London, George Allen and Unwin Ltd., 1950, P.11.
5. Cf. "Tasawwuf", op. cit.; also cf. Q. 2. 109, 164f., 177, 182, 186; 3. 31, 123 f.; 9. 119 f., 17. 1; 24. 35-42; 53. 1-18; 81. 19-25; 74 passim; 94; 96 passim.
6. Fazlur Rahman, Islam, Weidenfeld and Nicolson, London, 1966, p. 129.
7. Ibid.
8. Ibid., p. 130.
9. Cf. Hedayetullah, M., Kabir: The Apostle of Hindu-Muslim Unity, Motilal Banarsidass, Indological Publisher, Delhi, 1977, p. 31; M. Smith, "Rabi'a al-'Adawiya", SEI.
10. Sufism, op. cit., p. 43; also cf. "Rabi'a al-'Adawiya", op. cit.
11. "Tasawwuf", op. cit.
12. Fazlur Rahman, op. cit., p. 142.
13. "Tasawwuf", op. cit.
14. Nicholson, R. A., Studies in Islamic Mysticism, London, G. Bell and Sons Ltd., 1914, p.11; also cf. Fazlur Rahman, "Sufi Organization" in op. cit., pp.151-166.

15. Cf. Hedayetullah, Kabir, op. cit., pp. 68 ff.

16. Op. cit., p. 165; also cf. p. 201.

17. Cf. Hedayetullah, Kabir, op. cit., pp. 19f., n. 73, 76ff.

18. Hedayetullah, Muhammad, Dynamics of Islam: An Exposition, Trafford, Victoria, B. C., 2002, p. 186.

19. Smith, Vincent A., The Buddhist Empire of India, 3rd. ed., Oxford, [1919], p. 42; also cf. Baghi, M. L., Medieval India: Culture and Thoughts, Amballa Cantt., The Indian Publications, 1965, p. 221; R. C. Majumdar(ed.), "The Classical Age", The History and Culture of the Indian People, Bombay, Bharatiya Vidya Bhavan, 1951-60, 6 vols., pp. 29-33, 627-640f.

20. The Mystics of Islam, op. cit., p. 16.

21. Muhammad and Islam, New Haven, Cuntt., 1917, p. 175; also cf. R. A. Nicholson, "Ibrahim b. Adham", SEI,; H. Beverige, "Ibrahim B. Adham", JRAS., XL1, (1909), 751f.

22. Op. cit., P. 16.

23. Cf. ibid., p. 176; also see 'Aziz Ahmad, Studies in Islamic Culture in the Indian Environment, Oxford, Clarendon Press, 1964, p. 123.

24. The Mystics of Islam, op. cit., P. 17.

25. Ibid.; also cf. Zaehner, R. C., Hindu and Muslim Mysticism, Schoken Books, New York, 1969, pp. 93ff.; Muhammad and Islam, op. cit., pp.174f.

26. Revelation and Reason In Islam, George Allen & Unwin, London, 1957, pp. 90ff.; for the controversy about Abu 'Ali Sindhi's relationship with Abu Yazid and the former's influence on the latter, cf. Hedayetullah, Kabir, op.cit., pp. 36ff.

27. Quoted in Hindu and Muslim Mysticism,op. cit., p. 94; also cf. Revelation and Reason in Islam,op. cit., p. 95.

28. Cf. Chandogya Upanishad, 6.8.7, etc; also cf. Radhakrishnan (ed.), The Principal Upanishads, George Allen and Unwin LTD.,1953, second impression, 1968; The Mystics of Islam, op. cit., pp. 17f.

29. The Mystics of Islam, op. cit., p. 18.

30. Ibid., p. 19.

31. Arberry, Revelation and Reason in Islam, op. cit., p. 97; also cf. Essai, op. cit., p. 24; Fazlur Rahman, op. cit., pp.135ff.

32. Zaehner, Hindu and Muslim Mysticism,op. cit., pp. 119f.

33. Chaudhury, R., Sufism and Vedanta, pt. 11: "Some Great Sufis and their Doctrines", Calcutta, Prachyavani-Mandir,1948, p. 50.

34. Tara Chand, Influence of Islam on Indian Culture, 2nd. ed., Allahabad, Indian Press (publications), Private Ltd., 1963, p. 69.

35. Some of them were Ibn al-Arabi, 'Abdul Karim Jilli, Ibn al-Farid and Abu Sa'id ibn Abu al-Khayr who incorporated his ideas in their works; and Junayd, the renowned sufi, came to his defence, as did al-Hujwiri when he was accused of being a heretic.

36. For more information about Hallaj's preaching and teaching career which was almost fully determined by Indian ideas, cf. Hedayetullah, Muhammad, Dynamics of Islam: An Exposition, Trafford, Victoria, B.C., 2002, pp. 192ff.; Tarachand, op.cit., p. 70; also cf. Kitabal-Tawasin, op. cit., p. 129; Q. 2. 30; 4. 1; 7. 11, 59. 24; also see Radhakrishnan, op. cit., p. 515; Rig-Veda, 10, 121; Brihadaranyaka Upanishad, 1. 4. 1.; 1. 4. 3.

37. Cf. Atharva Veda, 10. 7. 7. 8; 11. 4. 13; Deussen, p., The Philosophy of the Upanishads, New York, Dovedar, 1966, p. 183.

38. Cf. L. Massignon, "Hulul", SEI.

39. Quoted in Chaudhury, op. cit., p. 58.

40. Cf. Kitab al-Tawasin, op. cit., p. 174. Massignon calls it: "I am the Creative Truth"; Also cf. D. B. Macdonald, "Hakk", SEI; The Mystics of Islam,op. cit., p. 79; The Idea of Personality in Sufism,op. cit.,p. 32.

41. Wim. T. De Barray (ed.), Sources of Indian Tradition, New York, Columbia University Press, 1958, p. 144.

42. Fazlur Rahman, op. cit., p. 136.

43. Ibid.

44. Ibid., p. 56.

45. Fazlur Rahman, op. cit., p. 153.

46. Ibid.

47. Hedayetullah, Dynamics of Islam, op. cit., p.198.

48. Cf. Arnold, T. W., The Preaching of Islam: A History of the Propagation of Muslim Faith, London, 1986, reprinted, Lahore, Ashraf, 1961, 2nd reprint, 1965, pp. 261-66.

49. Watt, W. M., What is Islam, Longmans Green and Company LTD., London, 1968, p. 137; also cf. Fazlur Rahman, op. cit., pp. 4, 55, 162f.

50. 'Aziz Ahmad, "The Sufi and the Sultan in pre-Mughal Muslim India", Der Islam, XXXV111, 1-2: (1962), 142-53.

51. Cf. Arnold, op. cit., pp. 280ff.

52. Cf. ibid., pp. 277 ff.

53. Khan, Q. H., South Indian Musulmans, Madras, 1910, p. 36.

54. Cf. Hedayetullah, Kabir, op. cit., pp. 88ff.

55. Op. cit., p. 222; also cf. K. M. Ashraf, JASB, 1, (1935), 103, ff.; Mujeeb, M., The Indian Muslims, McGillUniversity Press, 1967, pp. 10ff.

56. Quoted by Chaudhury, op. cit.,p. 129.

57. Cited in The Mystics of Islam, op. cit., p. 105.

58. Nizami, K. A., Some Aspects of Religion and Politics in Medieval India in the 13th Century, Delhi, Asia Publishing House, 1961, p. 263.

59. Cf. Humayun Kabir, "Islam in India", The Cultural Heritage of India, ed. H. Bhattacharya, 4 vols., Calcutta, The Asia Publishing House, (1956), 11, 581; S. M. Ikram, Muslim Civilization in India, New York, Columbia University Press, 1964, p. 131; C. C. Mackenzie, "Marriage Ceremonies of Hindus and Mohammedans in South India", JRAS, (1833), pp. 170ff.

60. Cf. De Barry, op. Cit., p. 510.

61. Cf. Sen, K. M., <u>Medieval Mysticism of India</u>, London, Luzac, 1929-30, p. 36.

62. Macdonald, P. B. "Emotionalism in Islam as affected by Music and Singing", <u>JRAS.</u>, XXX111, pt. 1; (1901), 195-252; pt. 11: 705-748.

63. <u>Op. cit.</u>, p. 83. There were seventeen <u>Sufi</u> orders functioning in India during 15th and 16th centuries, as mentioned by Abul Fadl, 'Ain-i-Akbari, Delhi, 1965, 111, 389-400.

64. Cf. Crooke, W., <u>An Introduction to the Popular Religion and Folklore of Northern India</u>, Oxford, 1926, 3rd. print, Delhi, Munshiram Manuharlal, 1968, 2 vols., 1. 47; also cf. K. A., Nizami, "Ghazi Miyan", <u>SEI</u>; D. S. Margoliauth, "Panj Pir", <u>SEI</u>; J. Beanes, "The Saint Pir Badar", <u>JRAS</u>, N. S., XXV1 (1894), 838-40; T. W. Arnold, "Saints and Martyrs (Muhammadan in India), <u>Encyclopedia of Religion and Ethics</u>, X1(1020), 68-73; Titus, M. T., <u>Indian Islam: A Religious History of Islam in India</u>, Bombay, Oxford University Press, 193o, p. 139; Macnical, N., <u>The Living Religions of the Indian People</u>, London, Student Christian Movement Press, 1934, p. 141.

65. Cf. Westcott, G. H., <u>Kabir and Kabir Panthi</u>, 2nd. ed., Calcutta, Sunil Gupta, 1953, p. 2.

66. <u>Op. cit.</u>, p. 172.

67. Nizami, <u>op. Cit.</u>, p. 262.

68. W. Haig (ed.), <u>The Cambridge History of India</u>. 111, London, p. 568, cited by 'Abdul Qadir in <u>The Legacy of India</u>, Oxford, Garett, G. T.,1938, p. 289.

69. Cf. Hidayet Hossain, "Fara'diya", <u>SEI</u>.

70. See Hedayetullah, M., <u>Sayyid Ahmad: A Study of the Religious Reform Movement of Sayyid Ahmad of Rae Barali</u>, Lahore, Sh. Muhammad Ashraf, 1970, pp. especially, 77-119.

71. Hedayetullah, <u>Dynamics of Islam,op. Cit., p. 210.</u>

72. Fazlur Rahman, <u>op. Cit.</u>, p. 153.

73. Ibid., pp.163f.; also cf. Stewart, op. cit., pp. 187ff.; Watt, op. Cit., pp. 36ff.

74. Fazlur Rahman, op. Cit., p. 161.

75. Cf, ibid., pp. 161f.

76. Op. cit., p. 163.

77. Ibid.

78. Hedayetullah, Dynamics of Islam,op. Cit., p. 214.

79. At present, there are several Muslim republics in Central Asia, such as Afghanistan, Azarbaijan, Dagestan, Kyrgyzstan, Tajikistan, Kazakhistan, Chacheniya, Tataristan, Turkministan and Uzbekisttan totaling a population of about 60 million people.

CONCLUSION

From our compact survey of Islamic Civilization, we have come to know the life of the Prophet Muhammad. It is well-known that since his father had died before his birth, he was brought up by his mother, then by his grandfather and uncle, Abu Talib. As a boy, he was unusual: thoughtful, rather than playful. At the age of 27, he became the Trade Representative of a well-known business lady, Khadijah. It is reported that during his business travels, he attracted the attention of his co-traders as a very uncommon young man who mostly appeared thoughtful rather than playful. Eventually, he returned to Mecca as a very successful trader. It was this practical aspect of Muhammad's life, rather than his family background, it is believed, that prompted Khadija of the age forty to marry Muhammad of the age twenty-five. In other words, it was a marriage of necessity rather than of love. As a family man, the Prophet had a few children but none lived up to the age of manhood. It is also reported that as a family-man, Muhammad had a few wives—a polygyny family man—but all of them were more like his Khadim (maid). However, he had one son, for sure, named Qasim; for that reason, he is known as Abu al Qasim (father of Qasim). That is why the Qur'an says, "Muhammad is not the father of any man among you, but he is the messenger of Allah and the Seal of the Prophets; and Allah is aware of all things" (33. 40).

Apart from this family life, Muhammad was a man of an uncommon life-style. He had been mostly a thoughtful and meditative man, as mentioned above. It is this aspect of his life in particular that prompted him to go to the top of the Mount Hira to meditate.

It was during one of those meditative periods that he received the first revelation of the Qur'an (Sura 97) which caused trembling and fever in him so that he rushed to his wife asking, "Wrap me, wrap me." She asked her uncle, Waraqa b. Nawfil, a Christian priest, to see him, and it was he who first recognised Muhammad as the Prophet of Allah. From that day in 622 C. E. the revelations came continuously until 632 on the Day of the Farewell Pilgrimage when the revelations ended (Q. 5. 2) totaling 6, 666 vs.

Following that historical event, the revelations completed the Five Fundamental Principles of Islam, viz., Unity of Allah; Five Times Daily Obligatory Prayers; Fasting in the Month of Ramadan (Q. 2. 183 ff.); Pilgrimage to Mecca only once in one's lifetime(Q. 2. 158, 189; 3. 197, etc.) and Poor Tax (Q. 2. 43). The Friday Congregational Prayer is an extremely important religious-social obligation like the Jewish Sabbath. It is important to understand that this weekly congregational prayer, usually held in public places or in a mosque, promotes Muslim communal unity, brotherhood, love, sharing and caring. For these reasons, the significance of the Friday Congregational Prayer cannot be exaggerated.

While the Prophet had been engaged in preaching the messages of the Qur'an, there appeared in the community opposition to the Prophet himself and to the new system of religion, Islam, he had been preaching and some people were getting converted to this religion. That situation resulted in open armed conflict. This phase of warfare, beginning from the Battle of Badr to the battle of Tabuk, the Muslims had to fight against their own people, save Tabuk, the Arab Bedouins, 68 military engagements—16 guzwa (commanded by the Prophet himself) and 52 sarya (armed clashes commanded by his companions).

On the other side of the field, The Prophet had to take extraordinary measures to organise his sahaba (followers) into an organisation—The Muslim Community (based on Unity, Brotherhood, Love, Sharing and Caring—*ummatul muslimin*). It was an extremely important measure considering pre-Islamic Arabian society—divided into clans, which encouraged enmity and infighting. Undoubtedly, this *ummatul muslimin* was the base on which the unparalleled united Muslim Community was set considering the pre-Islamic situation. This united *umma* crushed the Arab Bedouins completely, which resulted in the spread of Islam like wildfire all over the Arabian Peninsula. Thus Islam was established on the ruins of those disbelievers.

Although the Qur'an contains the basic information about the Muslim Community and its fundamental obligations, as mentioned before, more efforts were needed to establish this *umma* in the society with all essential rules and regulations to live a practical life-religious-social-economic, ethical and moral. This is done by the *shari'ah* (Muslim Law—the most comprehensive code for the *umma*). It should be stated that there are four Schools of Jurisprudence. Nevertheless, they are all in agreement as far as the fundamental issues of Islam are concerned. That means, a Muslim can follow fully or partly for performing the fundamental obligations of Islam. Minor issues usually are dealt with locally.

The next important component of Islamic civilization is the Muslim Family. A family is the basic social institution of which the mother is the base or foundation and the father is the guardian. This is an Abrahamic tradition which institutionalised it as the Number One Social Institution. The ideas of "mother-land" and "mother-tongue" are universally recognised and regularly implemented. In this line, the Qur'an says, "Man and woman are each others' support or raiment"(2. 187). That means, they are so inter-dependent that no family can function without their coordination and cooperation—in a broader sense, the whole society will come to a stand-still. By the way, the Qur'an also says, ". . . men are a degree above them"(2. 228). That is to say, man has the overall responsibility of the family as the guardian of it and the whole community, of course.

When we come to survey <u>Sufism</u> (Islamic Mysticism), we enter a different world. To discuss <u>Sufism</u>, briefly though, we have to develop a special understanding. In a nutshell, there is a well-known saying: Where the Muslim army conquered the non-Muslim territories, there the Muslim mystics conquered the heart of those conquered lands. That is to say, the expansion of Islam as a total system of life was due to the <u>Sufi</u> preaching—a preaching with a simple word: "There is no god but Allah and Muhammad is His Prophet." Once it is pronounced, the <u>Sufi</u> and the newly converted Muslims are brothers from the core of their hearts. It is a well-known historical fact that the <u>Sufis</u> scored their most important victory on the Indian sub-continent (now Bangladesh, India and Pakistan) by preaching their universal message of "equality and brotherhood" in a caste-ridden society. The "untouchables" of the Indian society, constituted a large portion of the population, and the <u>sufis</u> won their significant victory there with their simple preaching: "Whoever says there is no god but Allah, goes to heaven", and "All Muslims are brothers."

From this compact survey of Islamic civilization, we have come to know its essential elements. Islam is the closing chapter of the Semitic religion and tradition or culture with the Prophet Muhammad as the "seal of the Semitic prophethood", and the Qur'an is the last phase of the Divine Revelations; therefore, it is both important and interesting to know the developmental process or stages of a civilization. The Qur'an contains vivid references to pre-Islamic history with the names of many prophets before Muhammad, the "seal of the prophets", and a brief history of Islam as the follow-up and the closing chapter of the Semitic Tradition.

BIBLIOGRAPHY

1. 'Abdul Wali, M. K. S. "Hinduism According to Muslim Sufis", Journal of Asiatic Society of Bengal, N. S. X1X (1923), 237-52.

2. "On the Origin of the Chaktai Musalmans", JASB, LXV111 (No.3: 1899).

3. "Note on the Hari-Allah Sect", JASB, LXV11 (No. 3: 1898), 112.

4. 'Abdur Rahman, S. Bazm-i-Sufiyah. 'Azamgarh, Ma'rif, 1949.

5. 'Abid Husain, S. Indian Culture. New York, Asia Publishing House, 1963.

6. Abu Sa'id. Asrar al-Tawhid fi Maqamat al-Shaykh Abi Sa'id (The Secrets of the Unity According to theTeaching of Shaykh Abusa'id), com. Muhammad b. al-Munawwar, ed. V. A. Zhukovsky, St. Petersburg, 1899.

7. Agrawalla, N. The Hindu-Muslim Question. Calcutta, A. Chakrabarti, 1951.

8. Aiyangar, K. S. South India and her Muhammadan Invaders. Humphrey Milford: Oxford University Press, 1921.

9. Arberry, A. J. Sufism. London, George Allen & Unwin Ltd., 1950.

10. —Revelation and Reason in Islam. London, George Allen & Unwin Ltd., 1957.

11. Archer, J. C. Mystical Elements in Muhammad. New Haven, Yale University Press, 1924.

12. —The Sikhs: In Relation to Hindus, Moslems, Christian, and Ahmadiyya: A Study in Comparative Religion Princeton, Princeton University Press, 1946.

13. Arnold, T. W. The Preaching of Islam: A History of the Propagation of the Muslim Faith. London,1896, reprinted Lahore, Ashraf, 1961, 2nd. Reprint, 1965.

14. —"Saints and Martyrs (Muhammadan in India"), Encyclopaedia of Religion and Ethics. ERE X1 (1920), 68-73.

15. —(ed.), The Legacy of Islam. Oxford, Clarendon Press, 1931.

16. —'Attar, Farid-ud-Din. Tadhkirat al-Awliya (Memorial of the Saints), tr. A. J. Arberry: "Muslm Saints and Mystics: Episodes from the Tadhkirat al-Awliya". London, Routhlege and Kegan Paul, [1966].

17. Aziz Ahmad. Studies in Islamic Culture in the Indian Environment. Oxford, Clarendon Press, 1964.

18. —"The Sufi and the Sultan in pre-Mughal Muslim India". Der Islam. XXXV111(1-2: 1962), 142-53.

19. Baladhuri. Futuh al-Buldan. tr. P. K. Hitti: "The Origins of the Islamic State: being a Translation from the Arabic, accompanied with Geographic and Historical Notes of the Futuh al-Buldan. New York, [Faculty of Political Science of Columbia University], 1916.

20. Basham, A. L. Studies in Indian History and Culture. Calcutta, Sambodhi Publications Private Ltd., 1964.

21. Bearnnes, J. "The Saint Pir Badar", JRAS. N. S. XXV1(11894), 838-40.

22. Becker, G. H. "Djizya", SEI. pp. 91f.

23. Behari, B. Sufis, Mystics and Yogis of India. ed. K. M. Munshi, Bombay, Bharatiya Vidya Bhavan, 1962.

24. Bekeridge, H. "Ibrahim b. Adham", JRAS. XL1 (1909), 751f.

25. Bhattacharyya, H. (ed.). The Cultural Heritage of India. 2nd. ed., calcutta, Ramakrishna Mission Institute, 1953-62, 4 vols.

26. Blochmann H. "Contributions to the Geography and History of Bengal (Muhammadan Period"), JASB. XL11 (No. 1: 1873), 209-301; XL111(No.1: 1874), 280-309; XL1V (No. 1: 1875), 275-306.

27. Buru, R. "Kabir, Kabirpanthis", EKE. V11 (1914), 632f.

28. Chakrabarti, A. Hindus and Musulmans of India. Calcutta, Thacker, Spin and Co. Ltd., [1940].

29. Chaudhury, R. Sufism and Vedanta. pt. 11: Some Great Sufis and Their Doctrines. Calcutta, Prachyavani Mandir, 1948.

30. —A Critical Study of Dara Shiko's Samudra-Sangam (Majma' al-Bahrayn) : An Indo-Islamic Synthetic Philosophy. "Calcutta, Prachyanvani-Mandira, 1954, 2 vols.

31. Choudhury, D. A. "Calcutta, Prachyanvani-Mandira, 1954, 2 vols.

32. Choudhury, D. A. "Islam in Bengal", Muslim World. (M W). XV111 (1928), 147-54.

33. Colebrooke, H. T. "On the Origins and Peculiar Tenets of Certain Muhammadan Sects", Asiatic Researches. V111(1801), 338-44.

34. Cureton, W. "Indian Physicians at Baghdad", JRAS. V1 (1841), 105-119.

35. Dihlawi, 'Abdul Haqq. Akhbar-ul-Akhyar. Delhi, 1309/1889.

36. Donaldson, D. M. "Islam in India", MW. XXXV111(1948), 90-99.

37. Dvedi, H. P. Kabir: A Study of Kabir, Followed by a Selection from his Poems. 4th ed., Bombay, Hindi-granth-ratnakara Kayalaya, 1953.

38. Elliot, H. M. and Dawson, J. The History of India as told by its Own Historians. The Muhmmadan Period. London, Trubner and Co., 1866-77, 8 vols, reprint Calcutta, Susil Gupta, 1953-59.

39. Elphinstone, M. The History of India: The Hindu and Mahometan Period. 6th eds., London, J. Murray, 1874.

40. Enamul Haqq. "The Sufi Movement in Bengal." Indo-Iranica. XXX1 (1948), 9-32.

41. —"Sufi Movement in India". Indo-Iranica, XXX11 (1948-49), 1-12; XXX111 (1949-50), 11-4.

42. Firishta, M. Q. ibn Hindu Shah, Astarabi. History of the Rise of Muhammadan Power in India. tr. John Brrigs, Calcutta, Sunil Gupta, 1958, 2 vols.

43. Ghanni, M. S. "The Advent of the Arabs in Hindustan: Their Relations with Hindus; and their Occupation of Sindh". Proceedings of Indian History Congress (PIHC). X (1940), 402-410.

44. Goetz, H. The Crisis of Indian Civilization: The Genesis of Indio-Muslim Civiliztion. Calcutta, University Press, 1938.

45. Goswami, B. K. The Bhakti Cult in Ancient India. 2nd. ed., Varanasi, The Chowkhamba Sanskrit Series Offfice, 1965.

46. Grierson, G. A. "Bhakti Marga", ERE. 11 (1910), 539-51.

47. Grunebaum, G. E. von. (ed.). Unity and Diversity in Muslim Civiliztion. Chicago University Press, 1955.

48. —Medieval Islam: A Study in Cultural Orientation. 2nd. ed., Chicago, The University Press, 1953.

49. Gupte, B. A. "Acceptance of a Muhammadan as a Hindu Saint". JASB. L XX11 (No. 3: 1903), 87.

50. Halim, A. "Muslim Kings of the 15th Century and Bhakti Revival" (PIHC. X 1940), 305-310.

51. Hasan Ali, M. (Mrs.). Observations on the Mussalmans: Description of their Manners, Customs, Habits and Religious Opinions. 2nd. ed., London, Oxford University Press, 1970.

52. Hedayetullah, M. Sayyid Ahmad: A Study of the Religious Reform Movement of Sayyid Ahmad of Rae Bareli. Lahore, Ashraf, 1970.

53. Hesrat, B. Darashikuh:Life and Works. Calcutta, by the Author, [1953].

54. Hidaet Hossain, M. "Fara'idiya", SEI, pp. 99f.

55. Hitti, P. K. History of the Arabs: From the Earliest Times to the Present. 7th ed., London, Macmillan, New York, St. Martin's Press, 1961.

Additional Books:

1. "Hadjdj", <u>SEI</u>; Also cf. F. Buhl, "Tawaf", <u>SEI</u>; Ibn Hisham, Sirat . . . , 1, 51; Smith, W. Robertson, <u>Religion of the Semites: The Fundamental Institutions</u>, Schocken Books, New York, 1972.
2. Cf. <u>Exd.</u> 19. 19. 10, 14; 11. 15; "Hajj", <u>op. Cit.</u>
3. Cf. I. Goldziher, "Revue de l' Histoire des Religious", (R H R), xxxv11; also cf. Q. 2. 197.
4. Cf. G-Demombyne, <u>op. Cit.</u>
5. For complete information about the remaining ceremonies of the "Hadjdj", <u>SEI</u>.
    R. Parel, "<u>Umra</u>" <u>SEI</u>; Ibn Hisham, <u>op. Cit.</u>; also cf. Q. 2. 198, 203.
6. Cf. "<u>Tawaf</u>", <u>SEI</u>; Ps. 366.